Flowers

In Black & White

Photographs by Leo Touchet

Flowers
In Black & White

Design: Leo Touchet

Type: Garamond

ISBN-13: 978-1-7324433-3-4

First Edition
November 2018

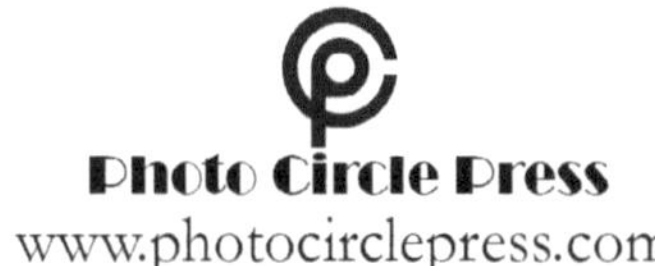

Photo Circle Press
www.photocirclepress.com

In memory of **David Wyland**, the Newsweek picture editor, who introduced me to the digital world, and helped me post my first photos on the internet at www.photoarts.com in 1998.

Film to Digital

For the first 30 years of my photography career I photographed with film cameras and spent many hours in darkrooms processing film and prints. I wasn't that concerned with the technical aspects of the films and cameras. I just wanted to capture what I saw as quickly as possible which resulted in many under and over exposed negatives. Making good prints from bad negatives helped me to became a good printer

As digital photography moved into my world, I realized that my clients no longer needed me to make their ugly facilities look good. The writer or engineer could simply provide the digital image to the graphic designer, who then worked his or her magic with Photoshop to get what photographers spend days trying to achieve. Learning this new medium wasn't easy.

First, I bought a small Olympus digital camera. Then I bought Photoshop software which I then had to learn to use. Compared to the hours spent retouching prints with a fine sable brush and spottone, Photoshop could accomplish the same in minutes.

I later bought a professional digital camera and began photographing flowers. With film cameras, I needed to use two cameras to shoot both color and black & white at the same time. This required me to think differently for each. It was like having a second brain. The digital camera offered both with the same camera. However, shooting both simultaneously still required a second brain. After a while, I realized I really did not like photographing in color. I'm much happier thinking in black & white.

With the help of Photoshop, I learned to convert the flower photographs into black & white images. I began to enjoy photography again. The images in this book are the result of my first digital project which went on for several years. I hope you enjoy these images.

Leo Touchet

Contents

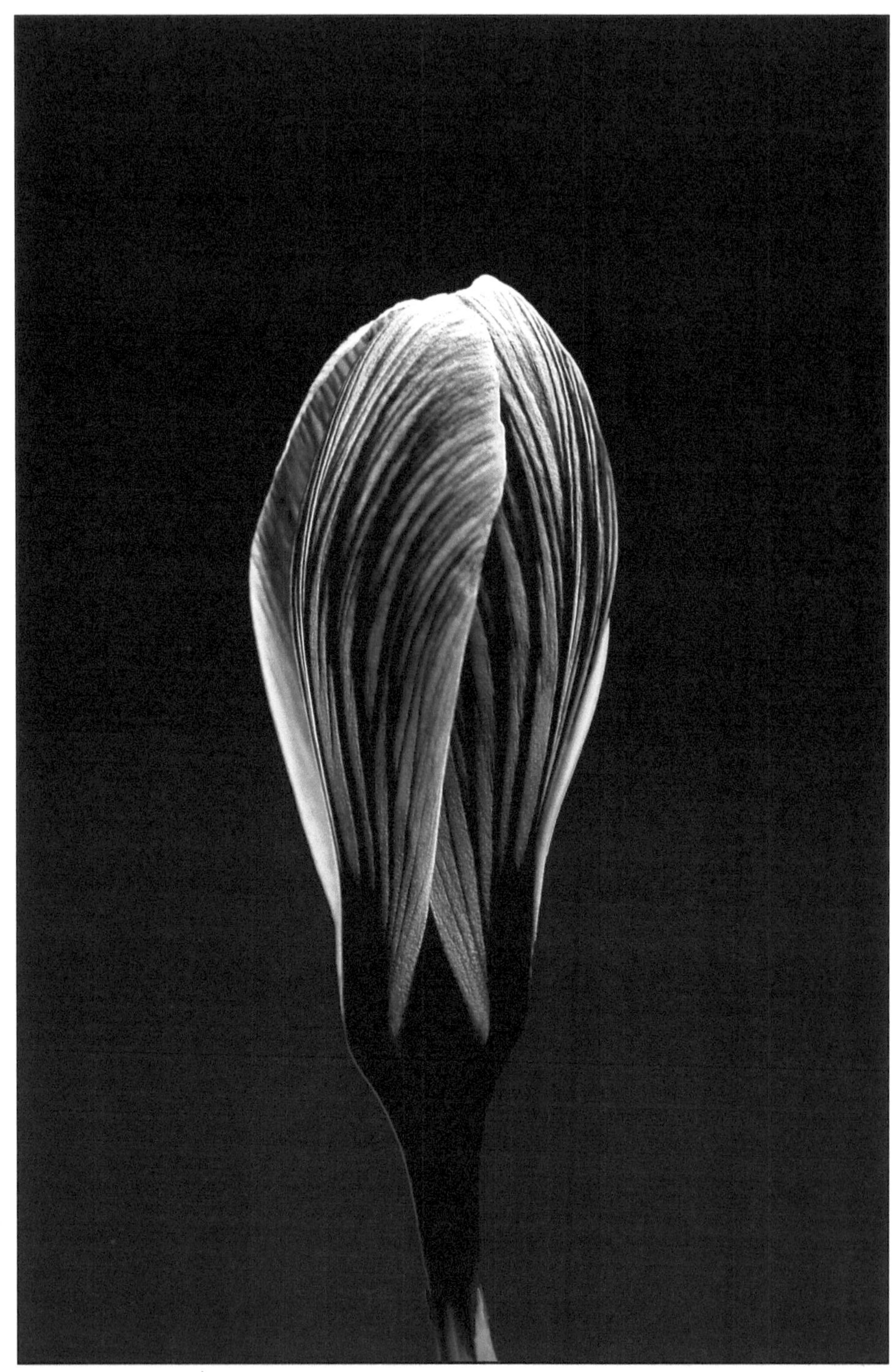

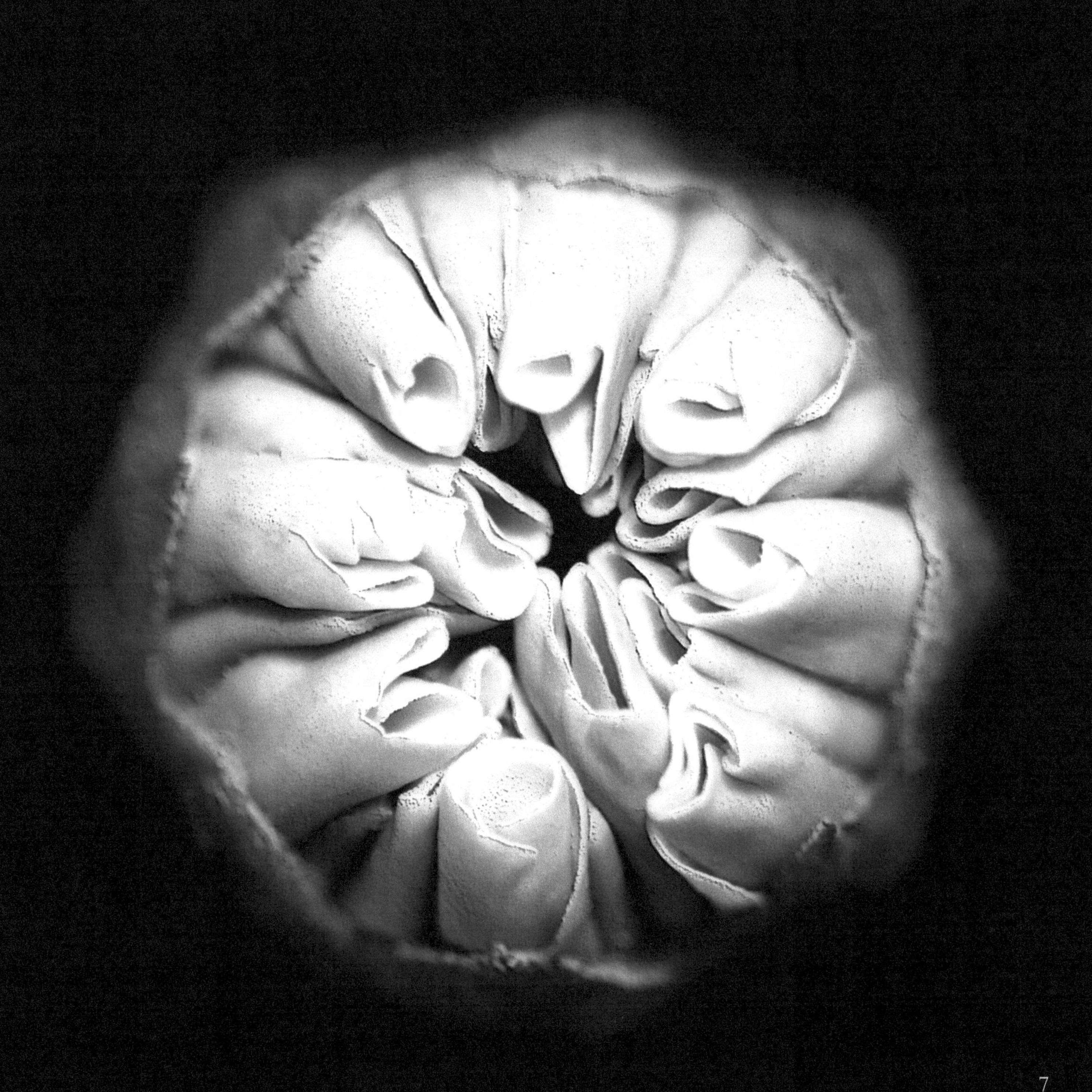

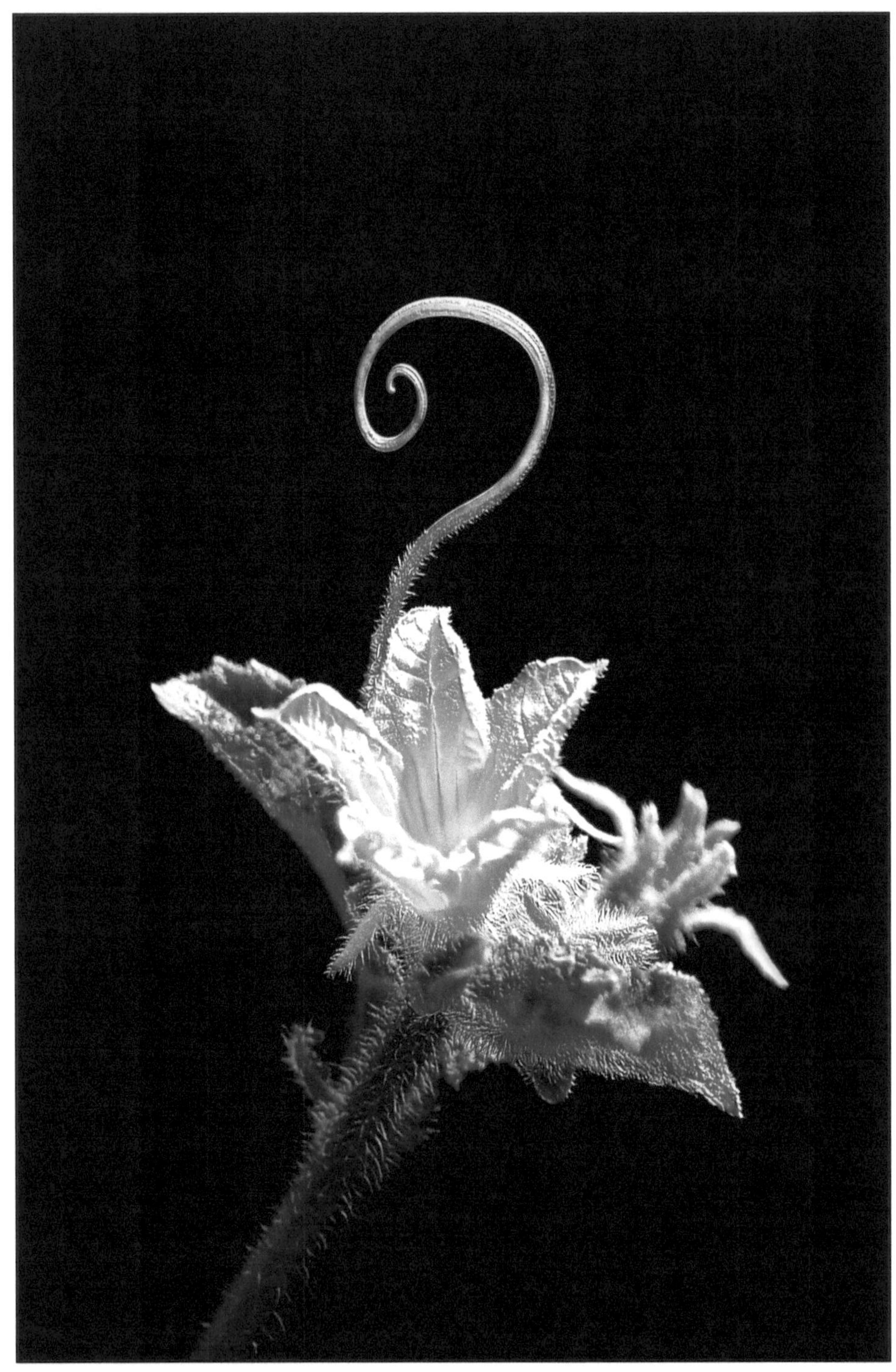

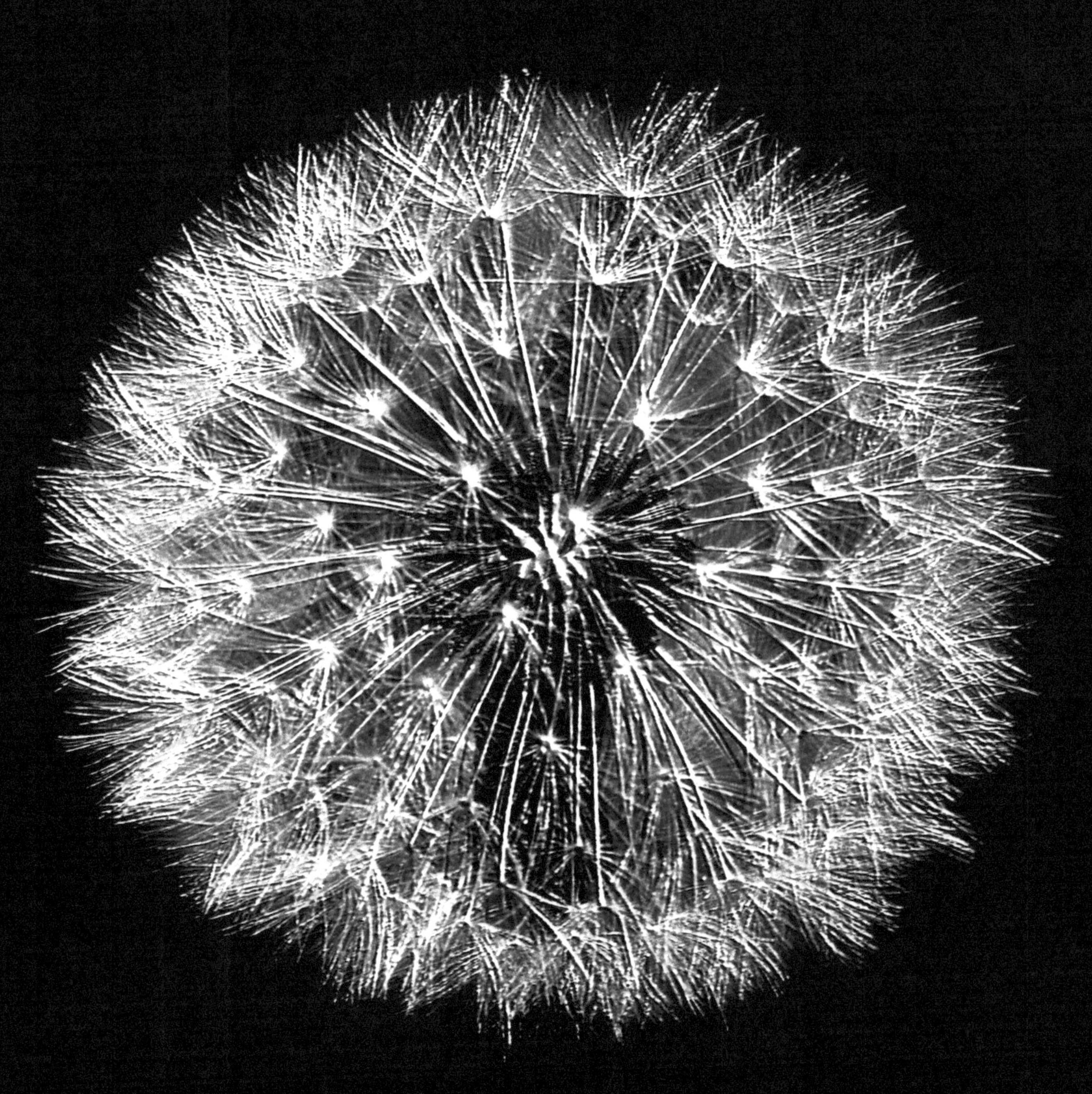

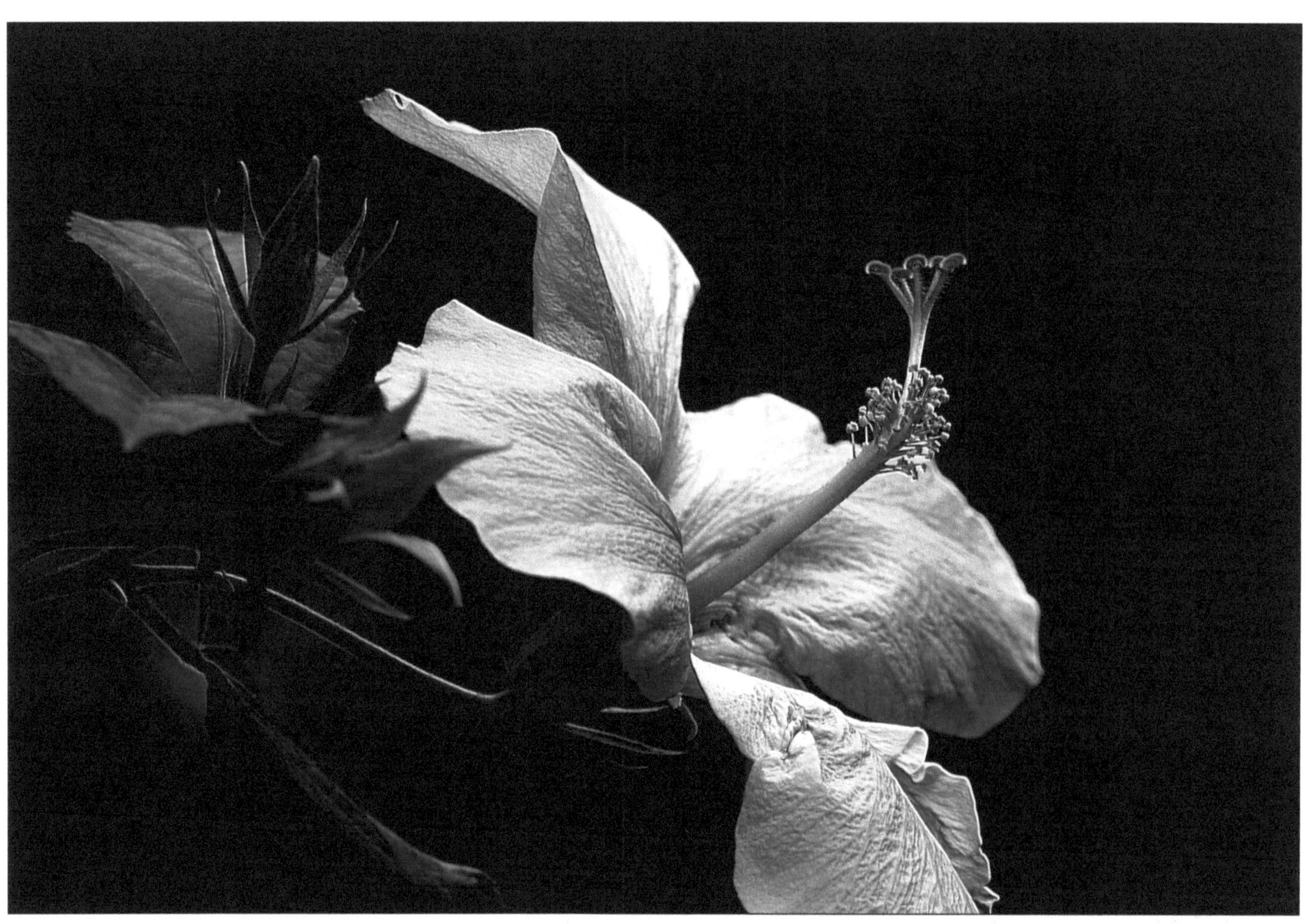

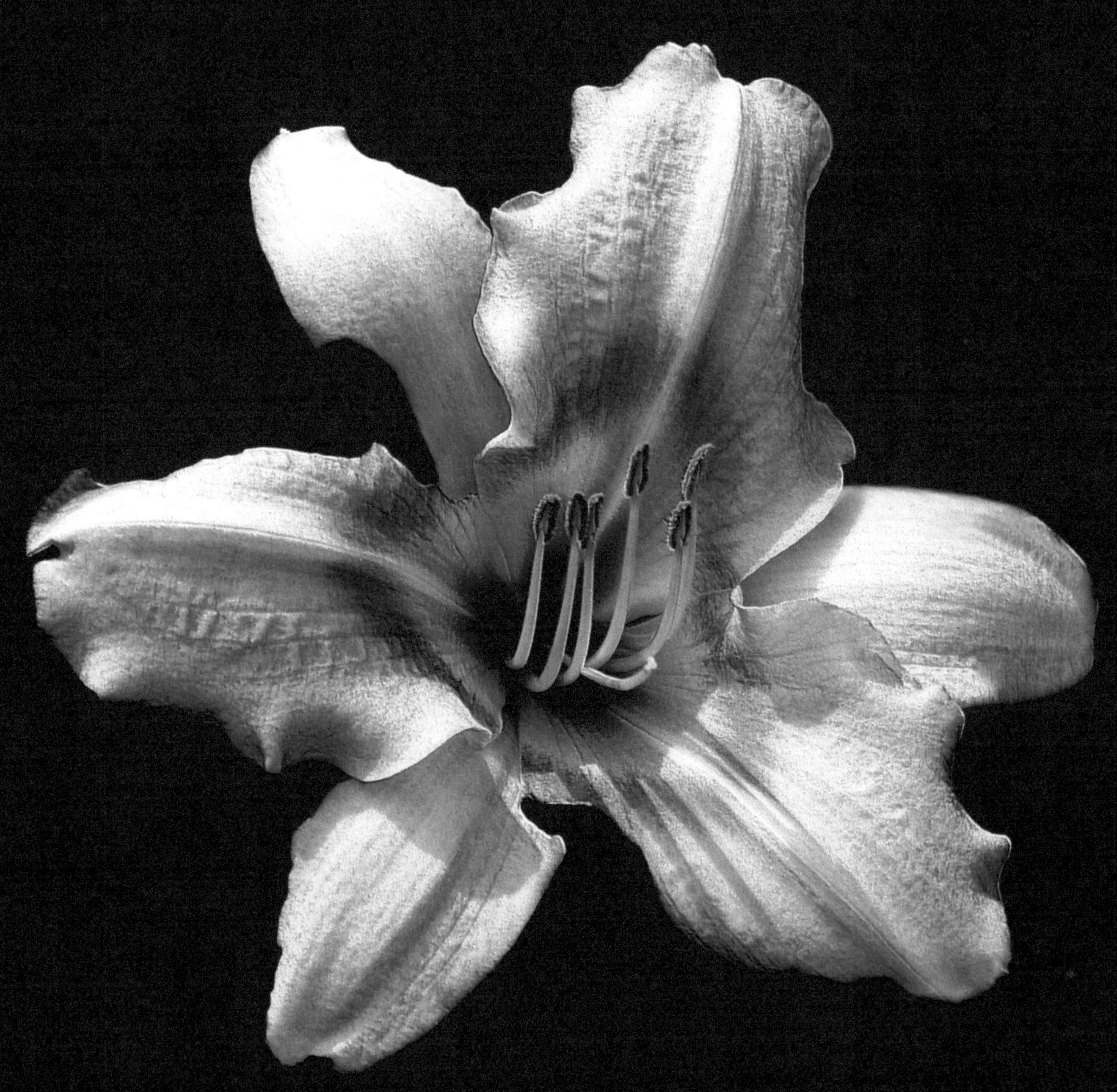

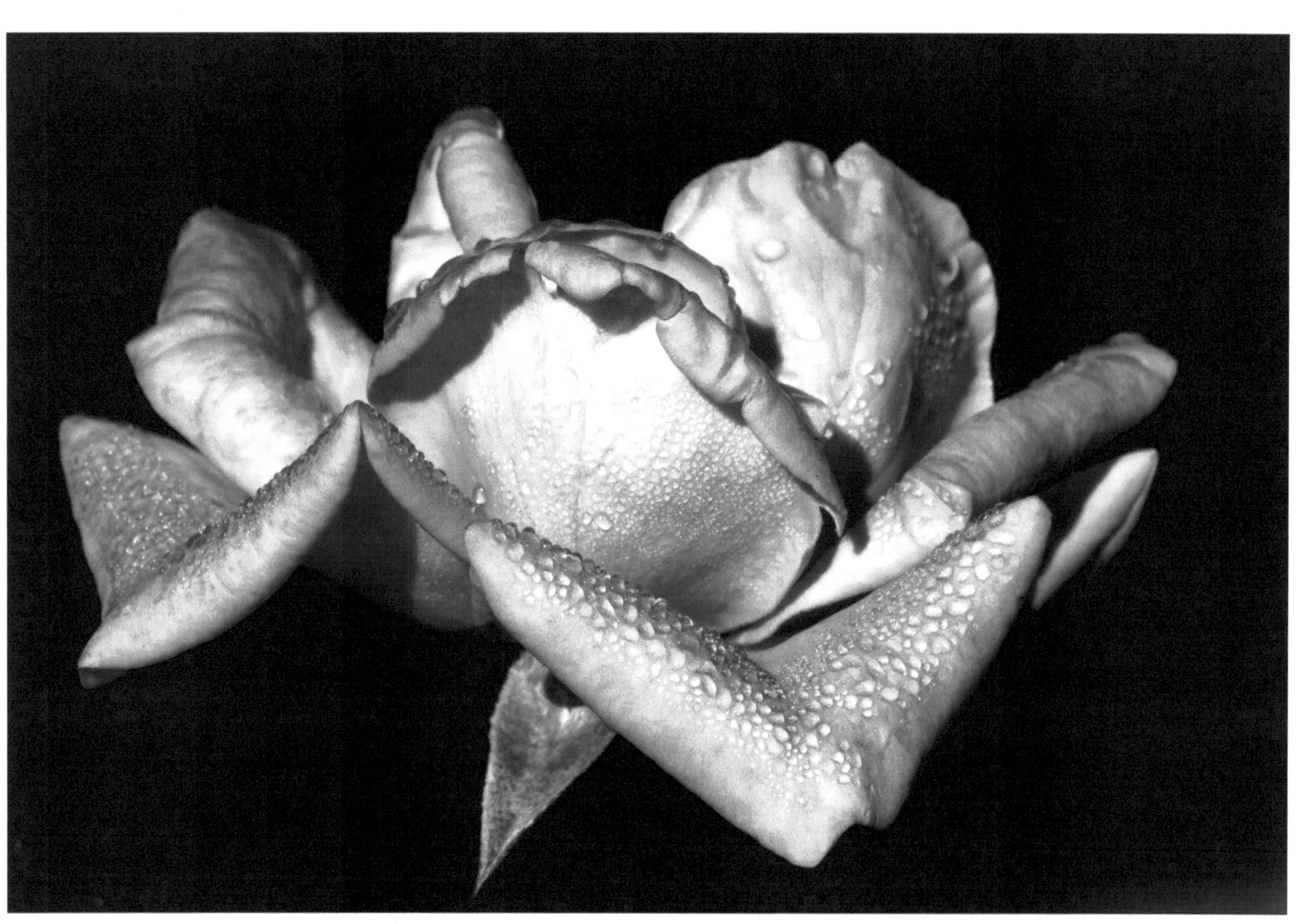

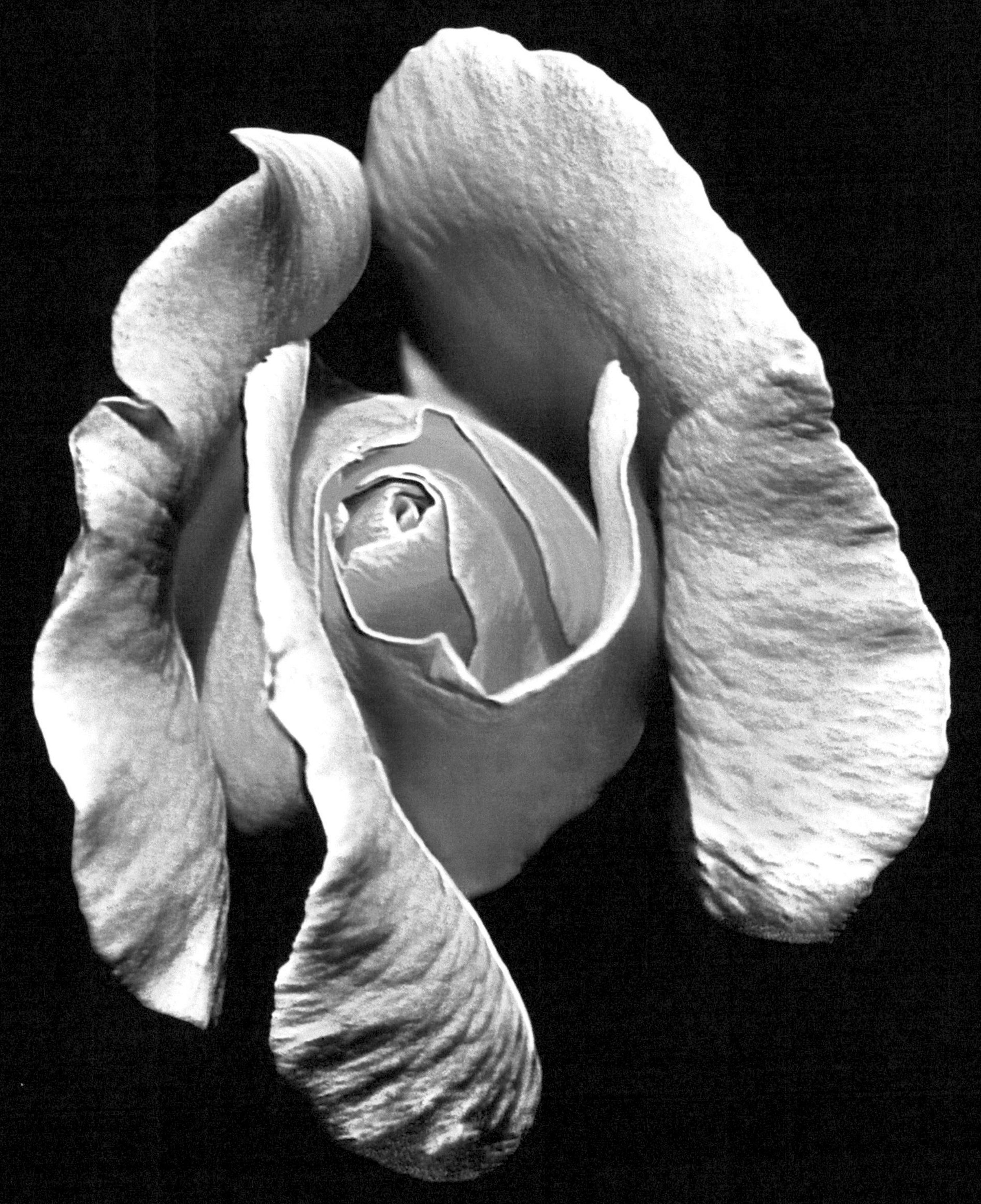

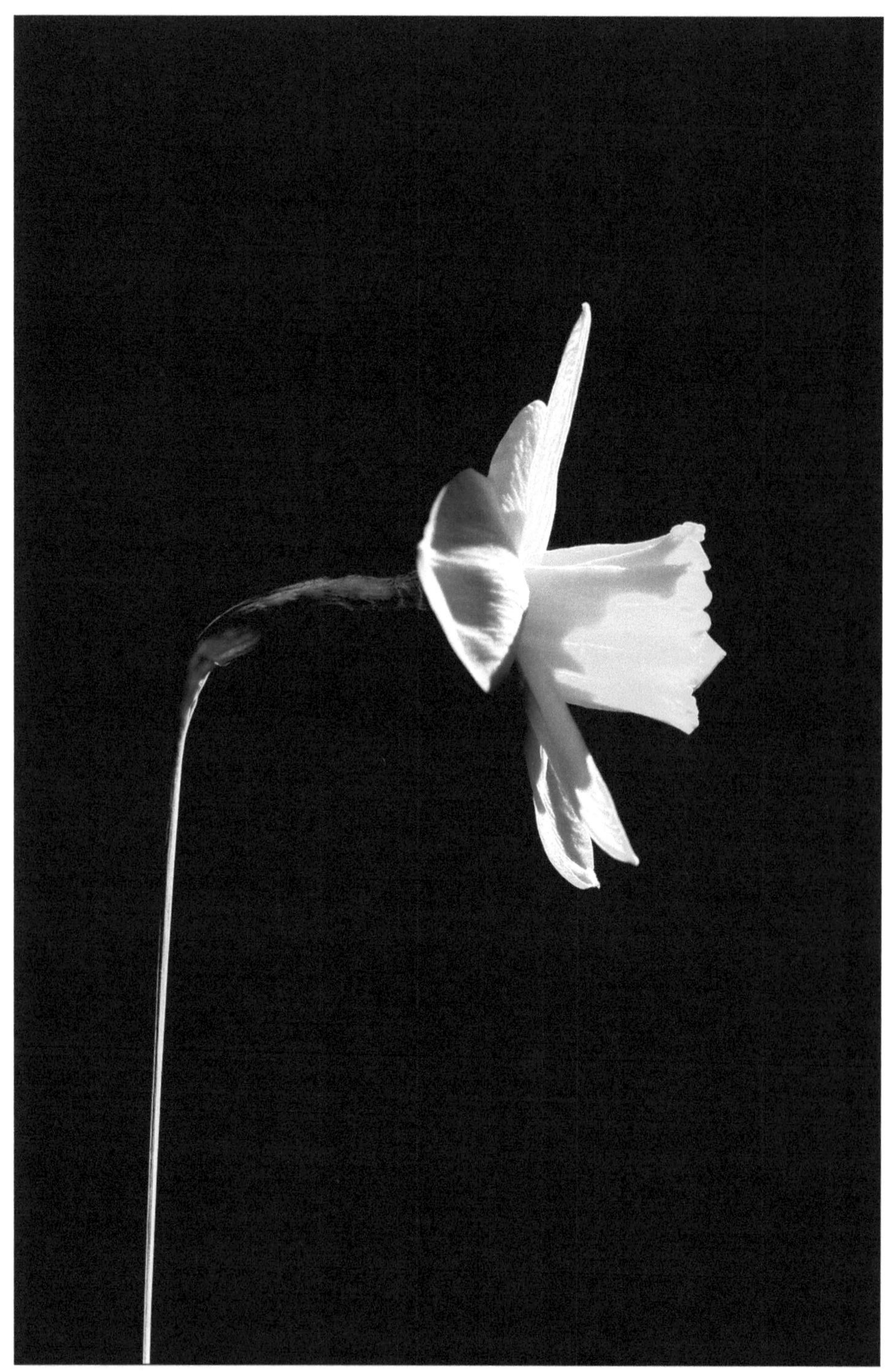

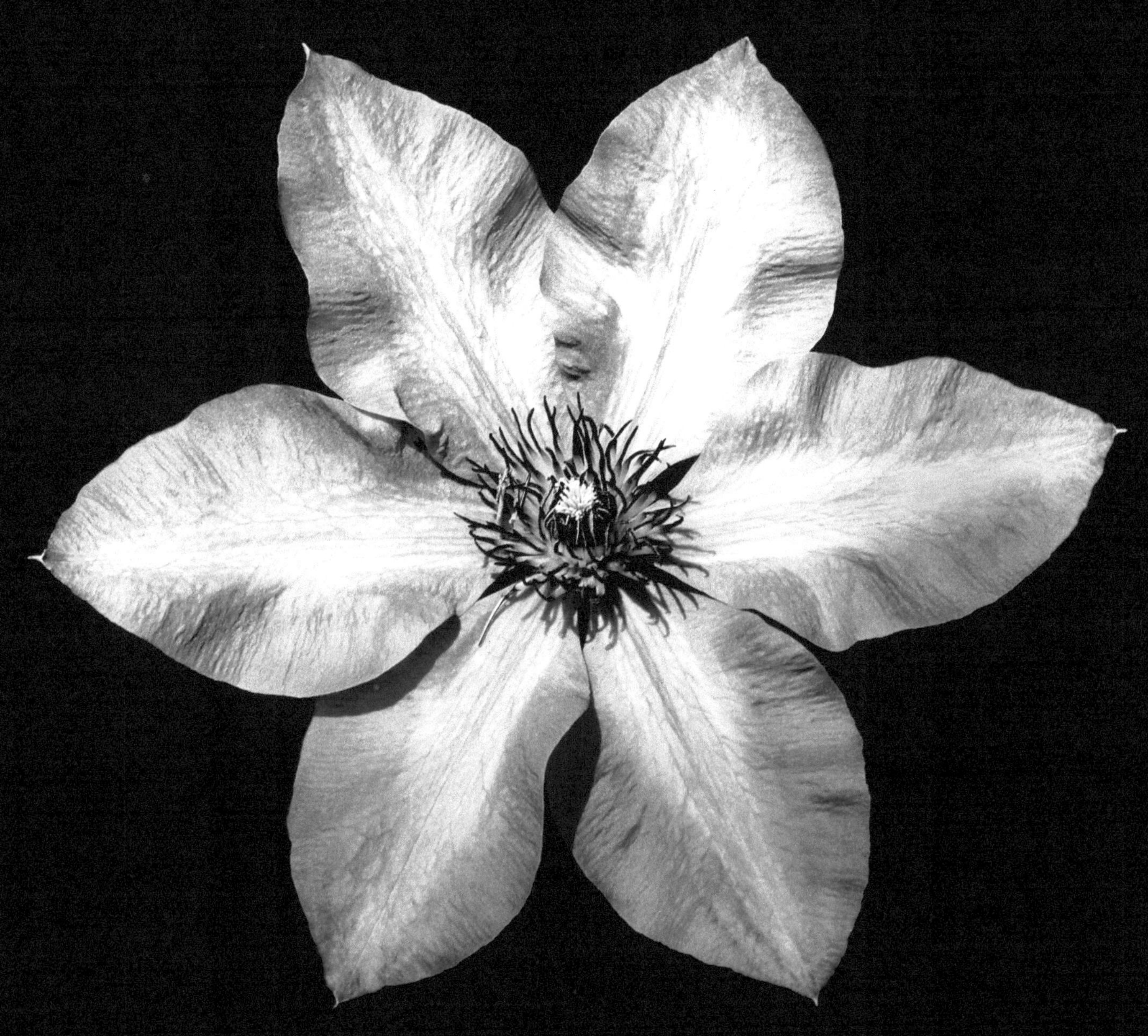

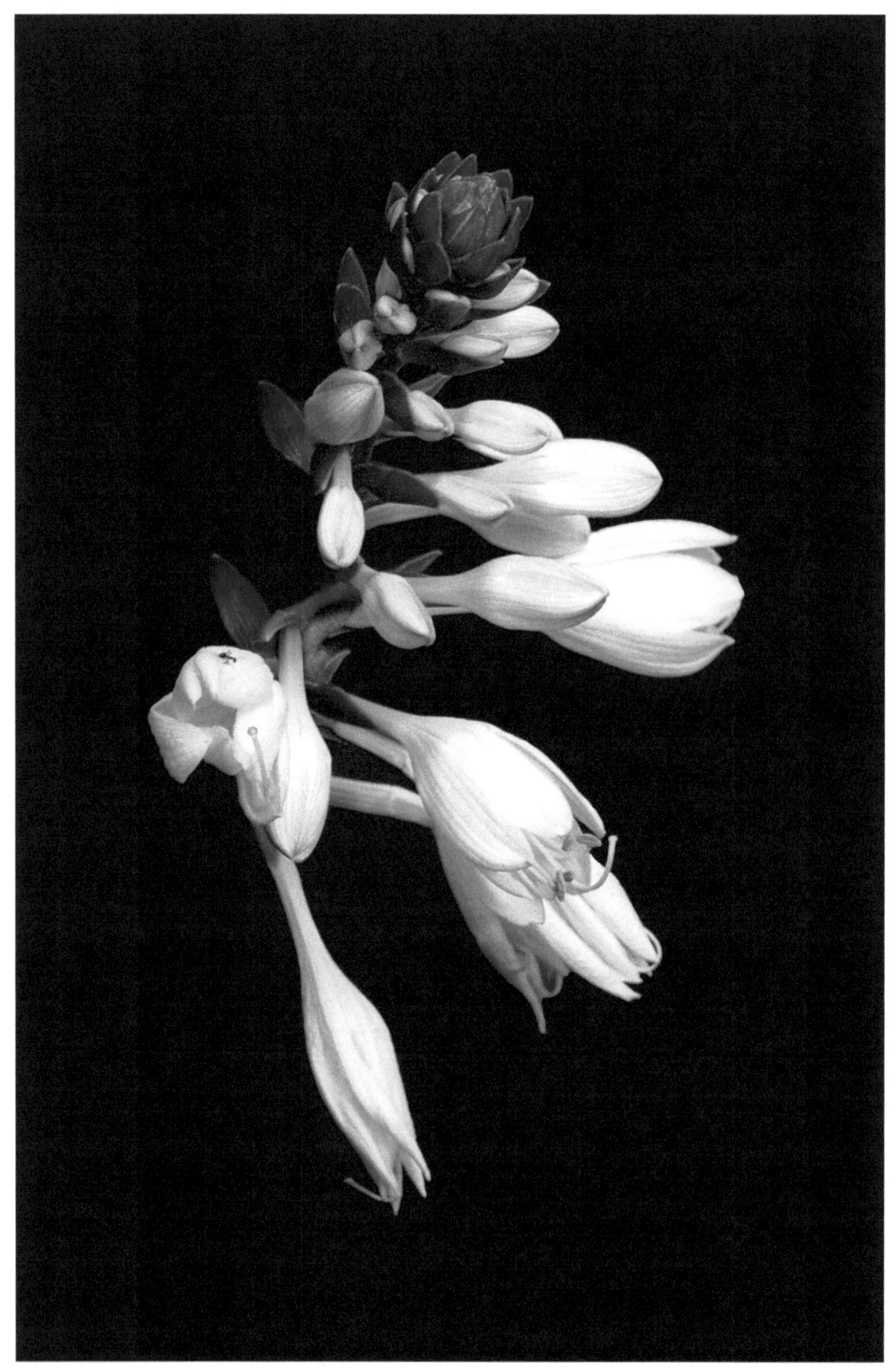

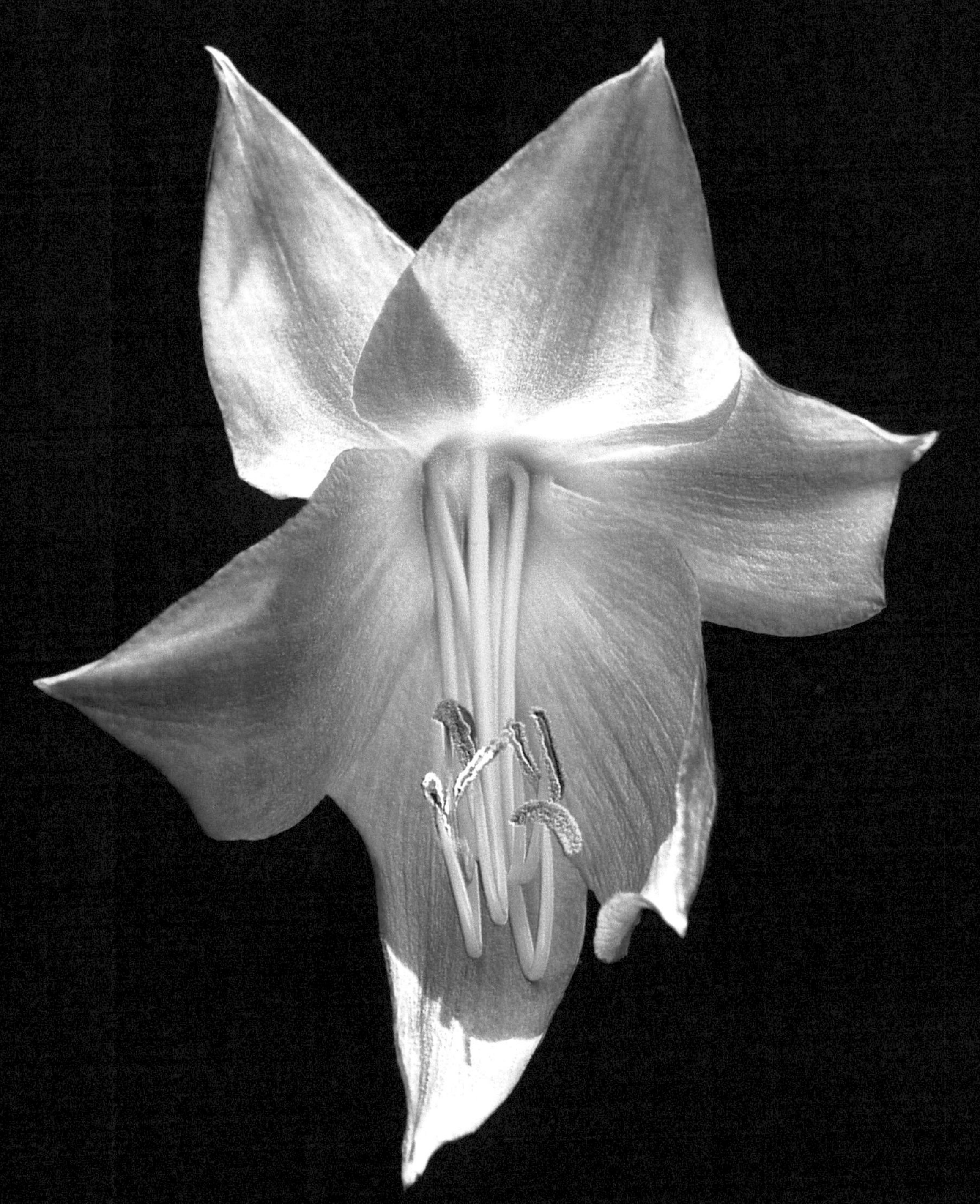

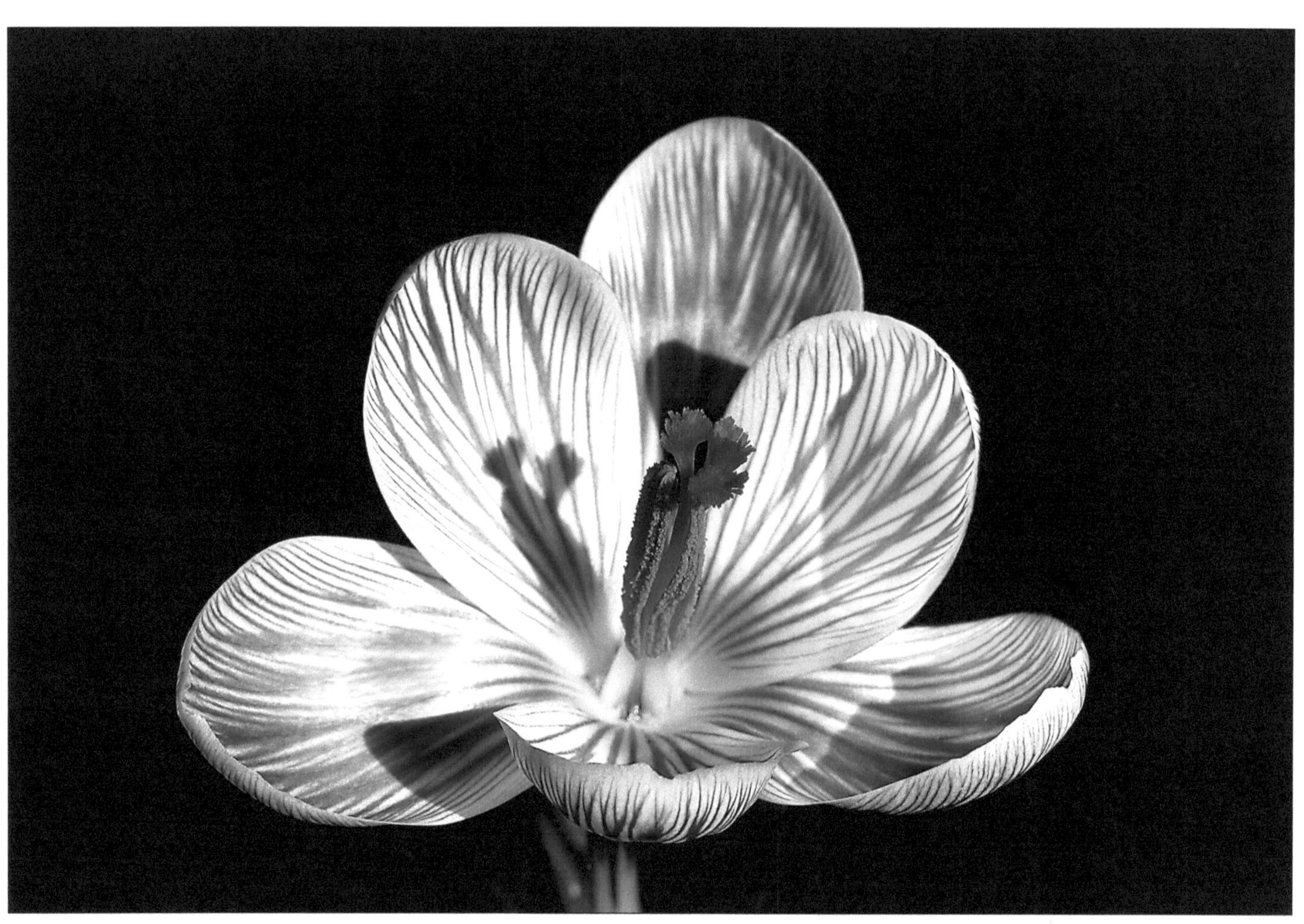

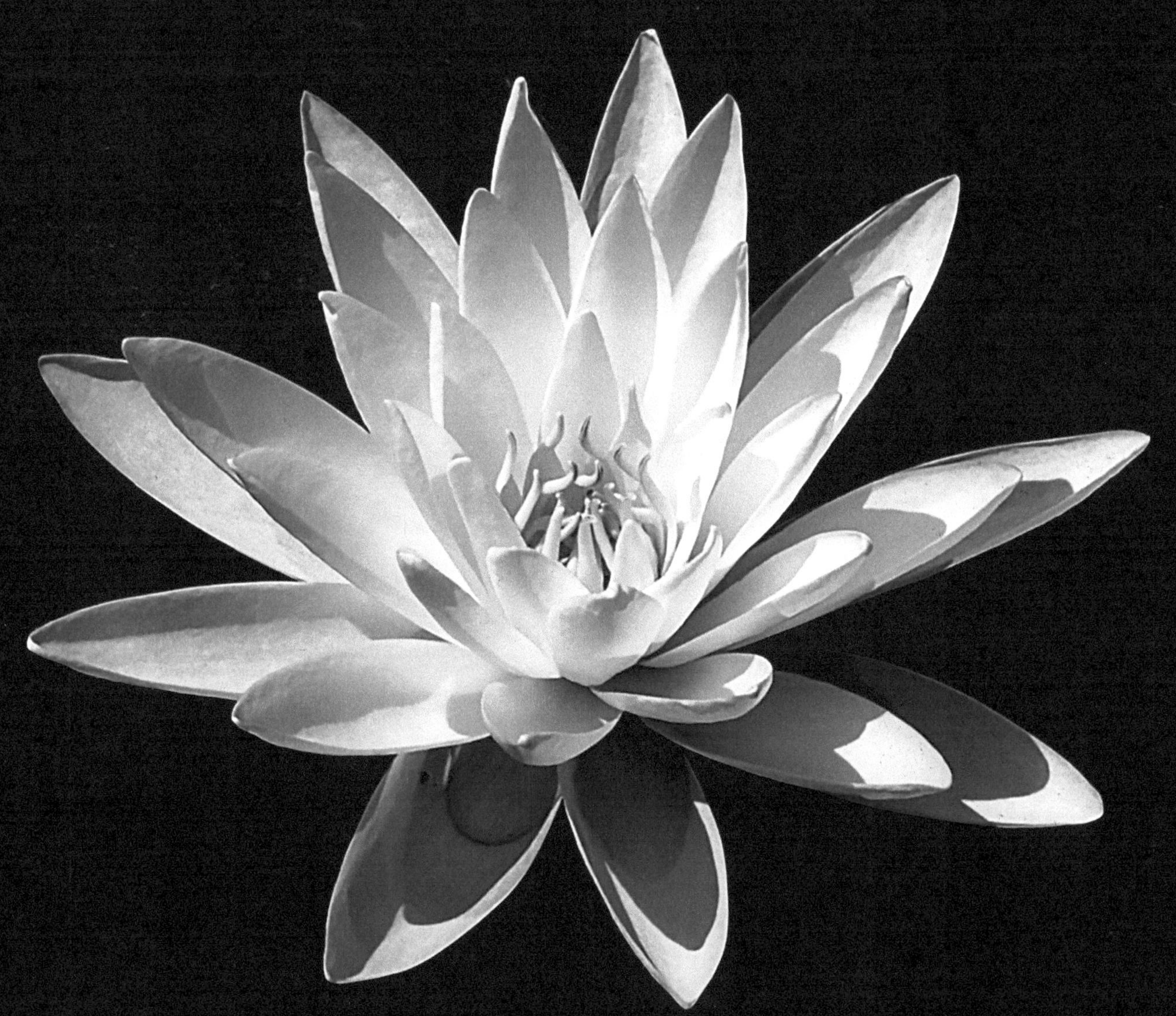

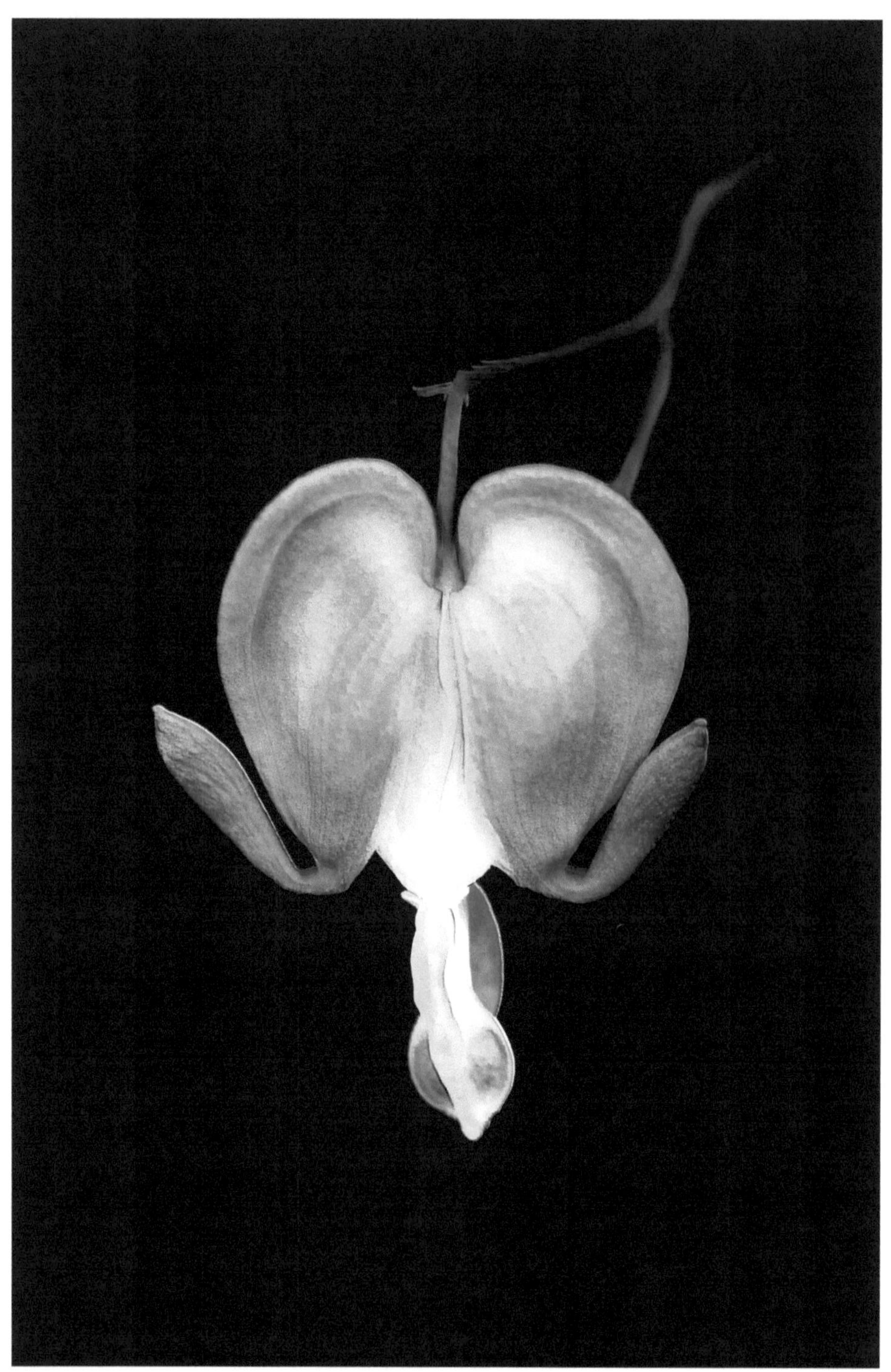

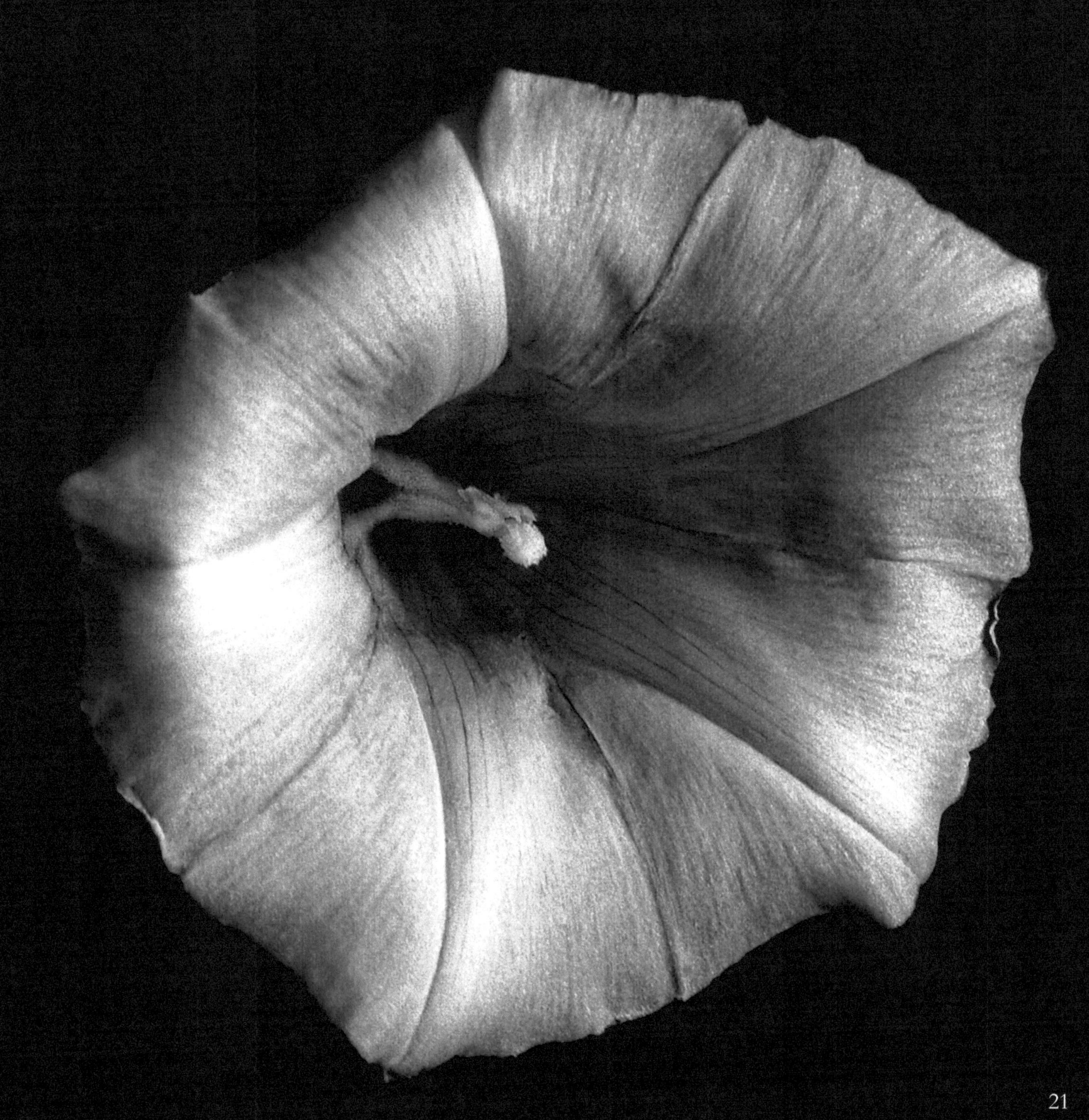

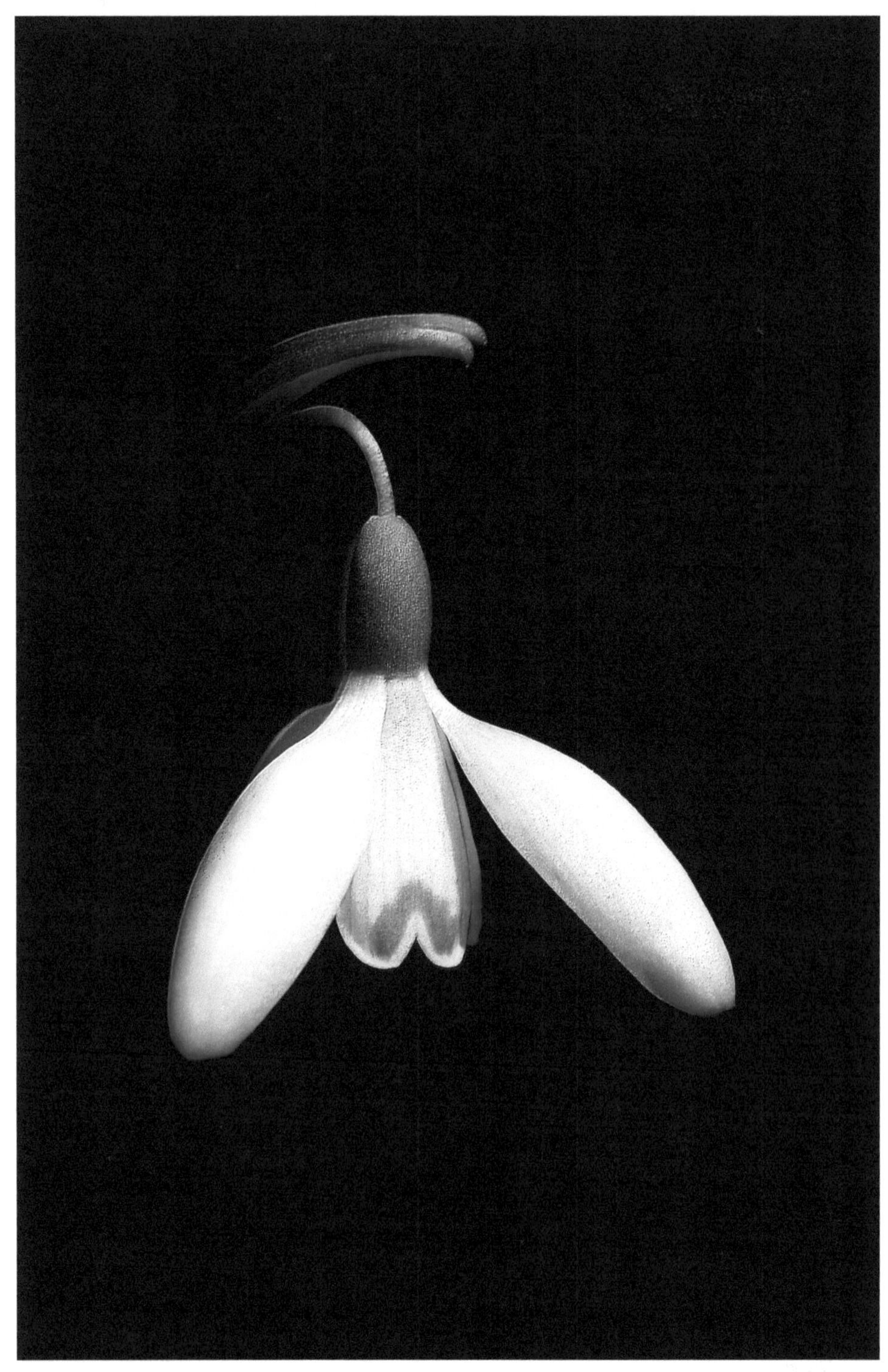

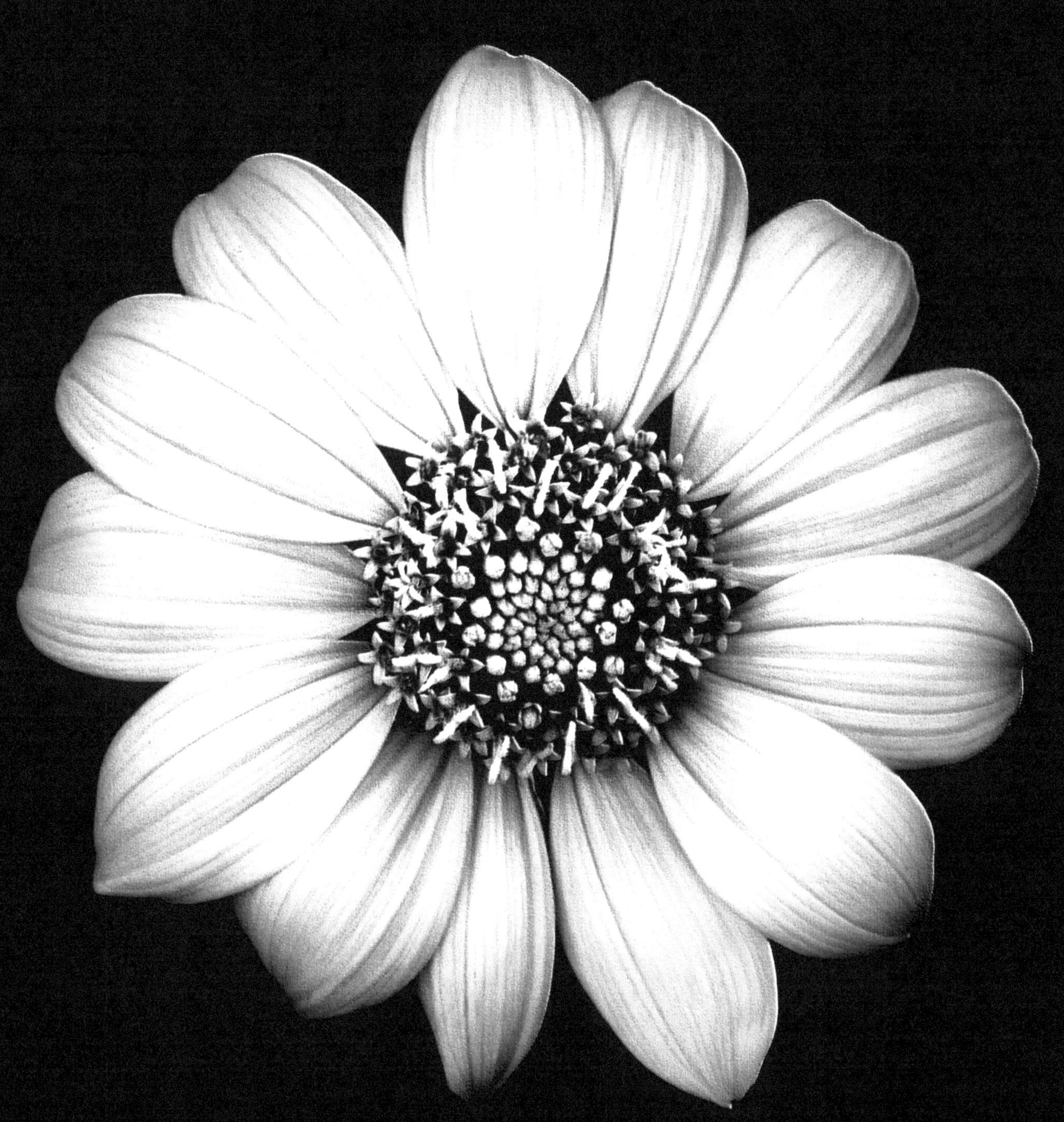

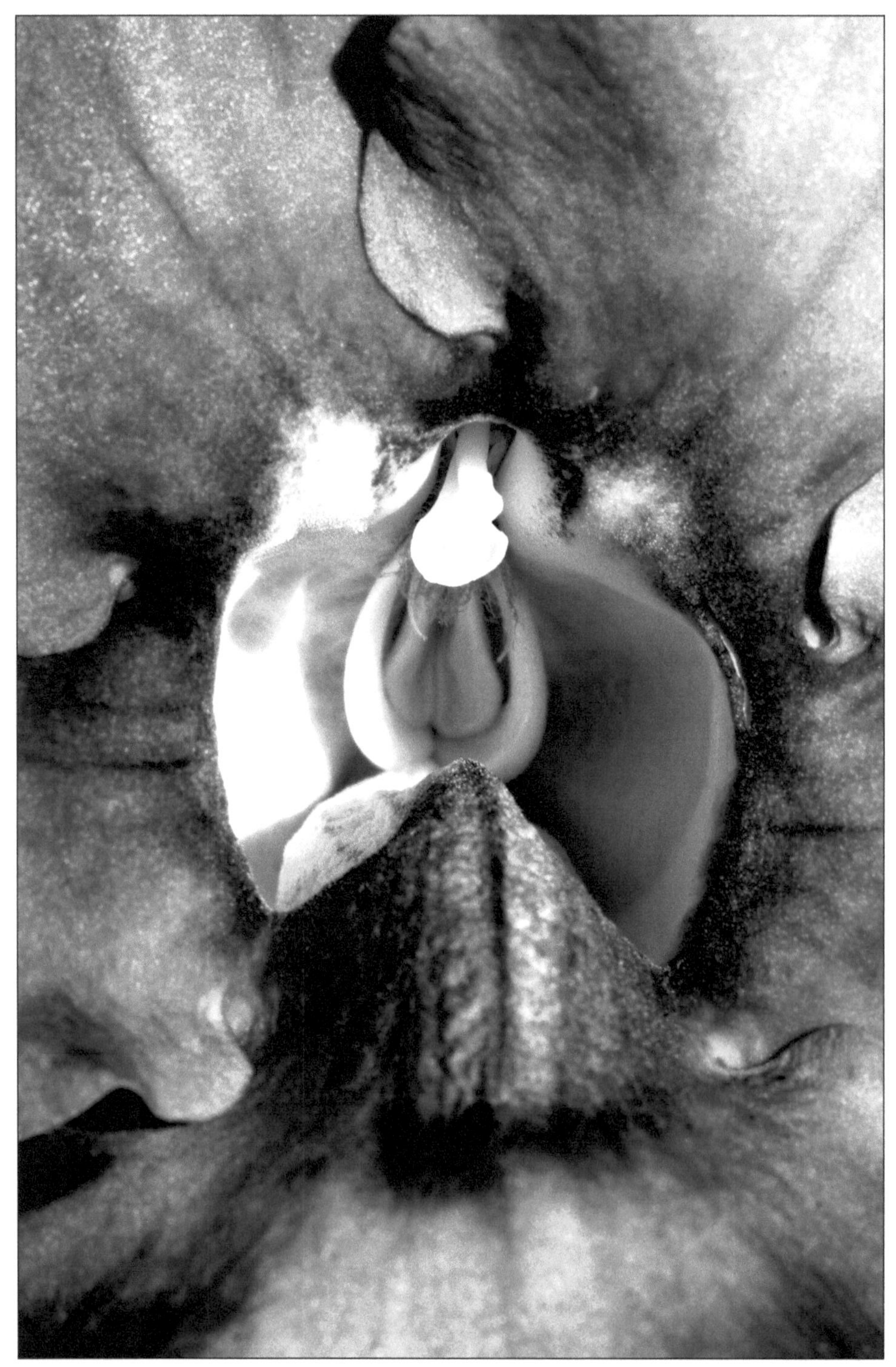

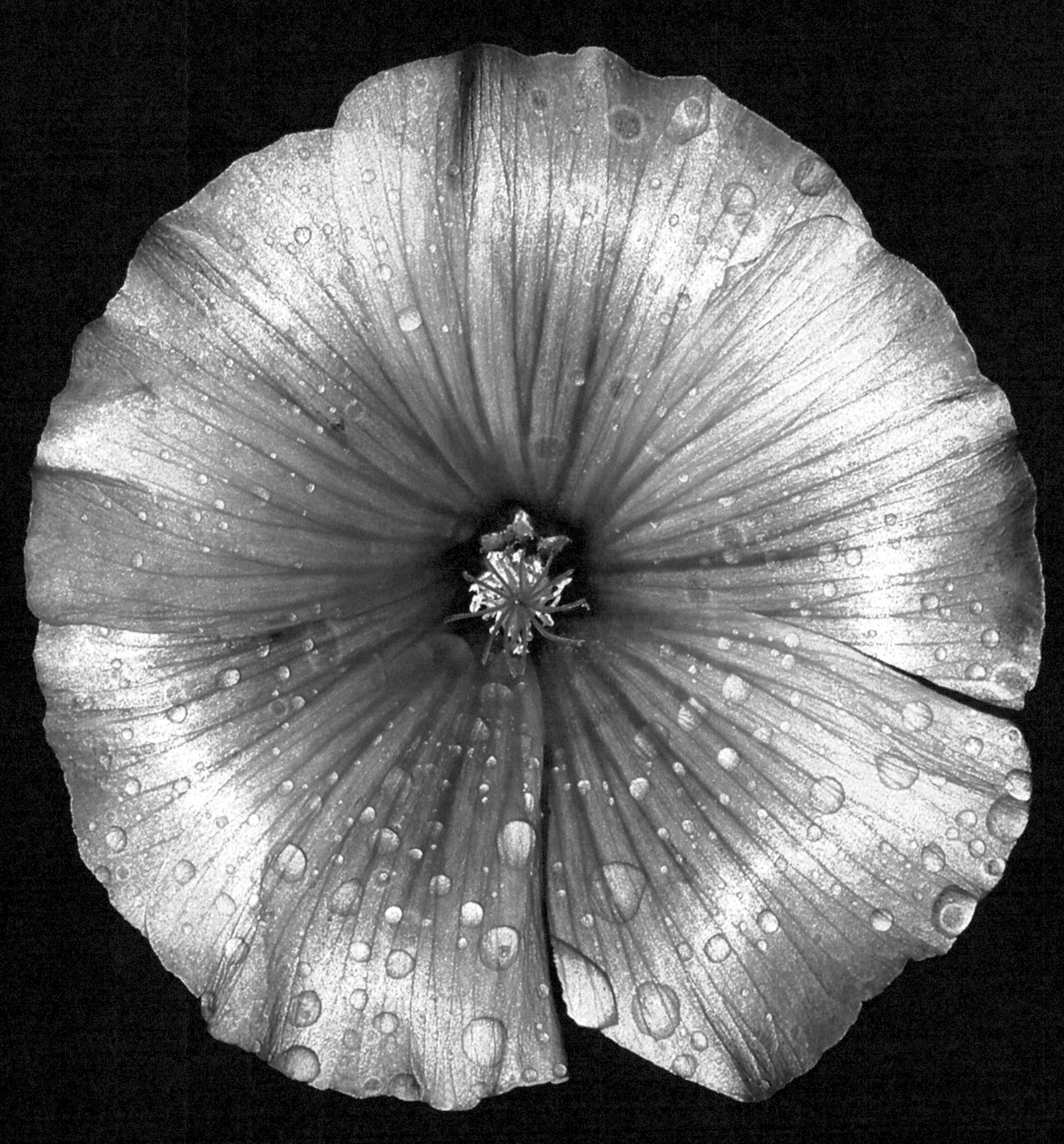

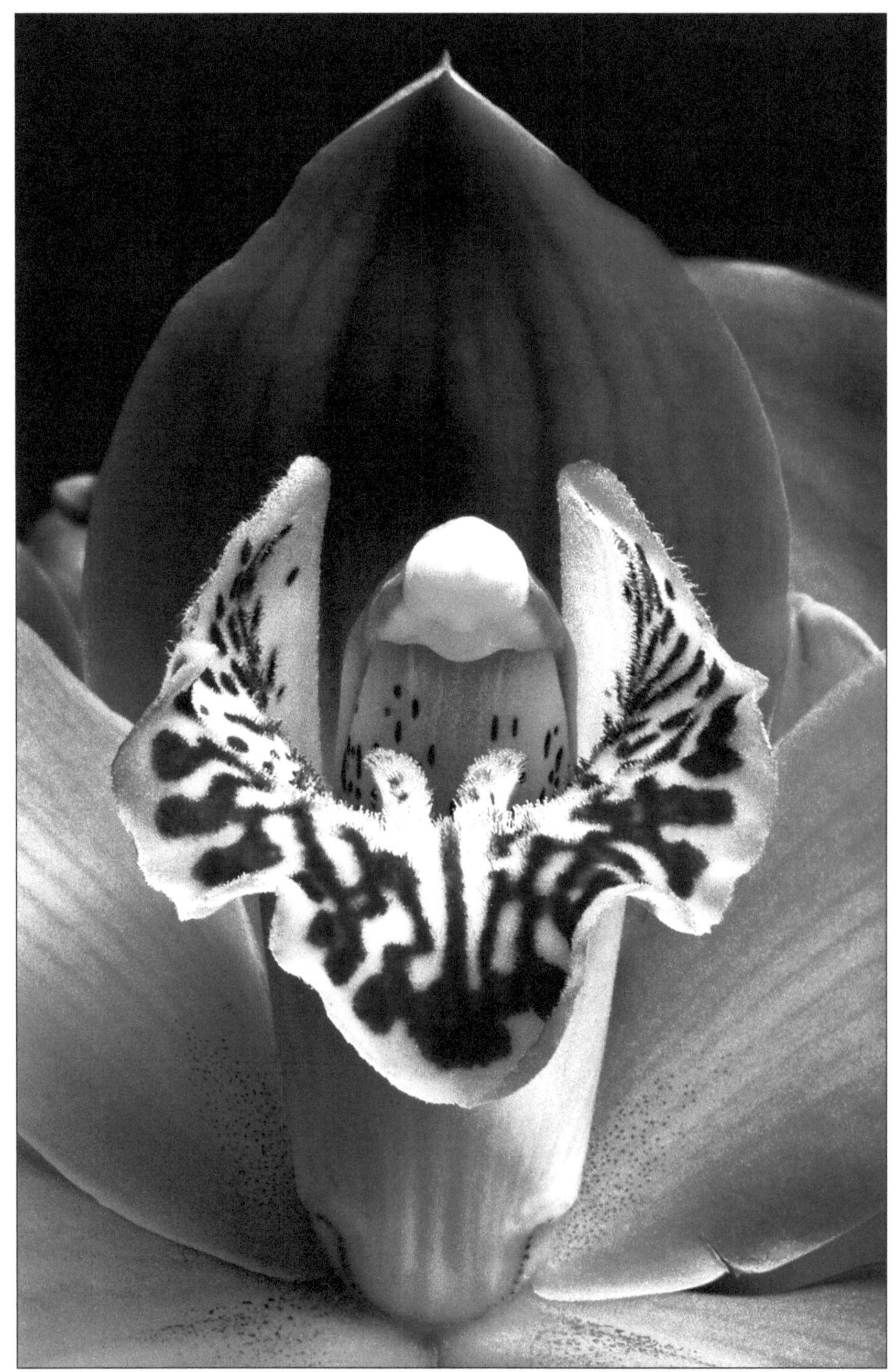

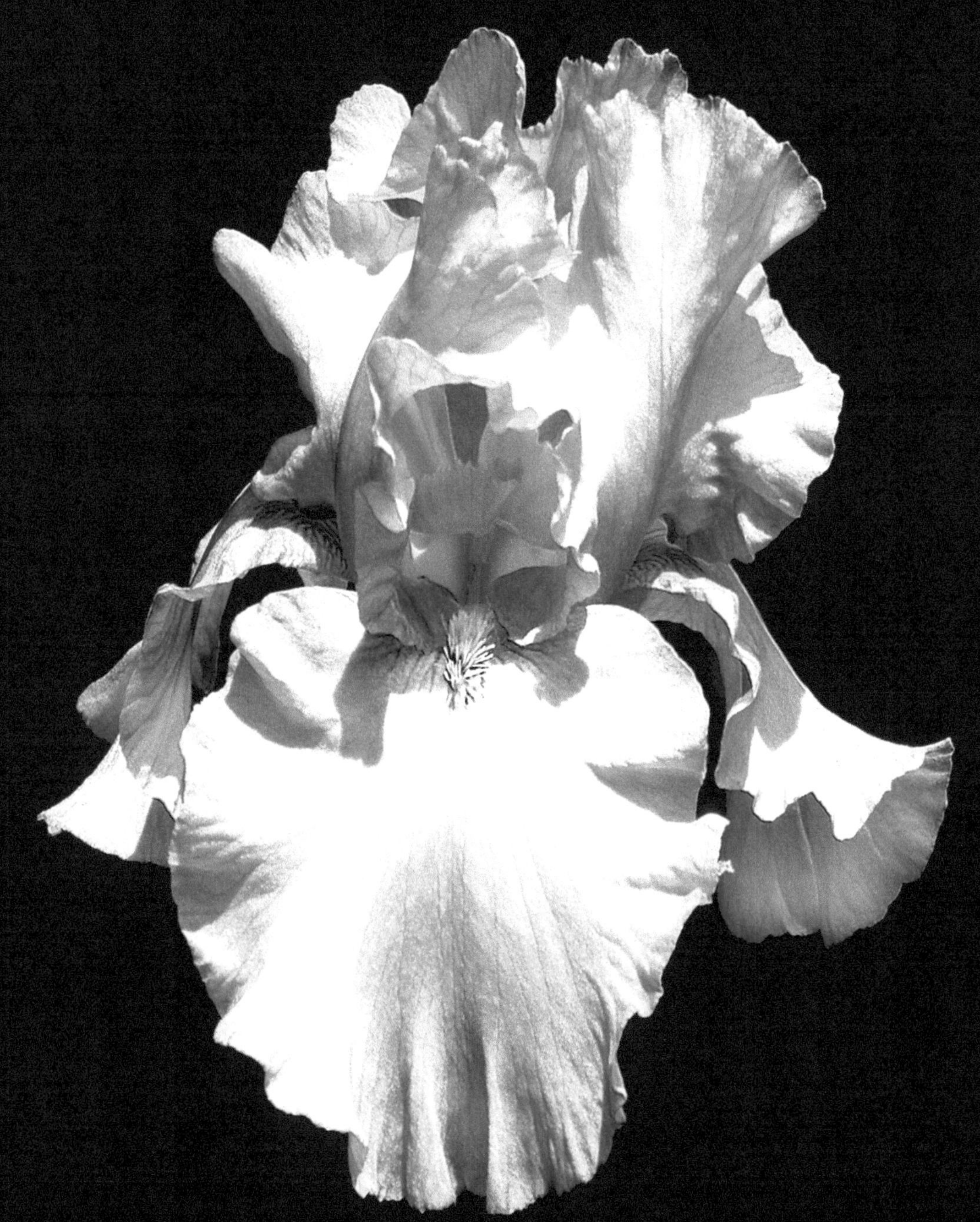

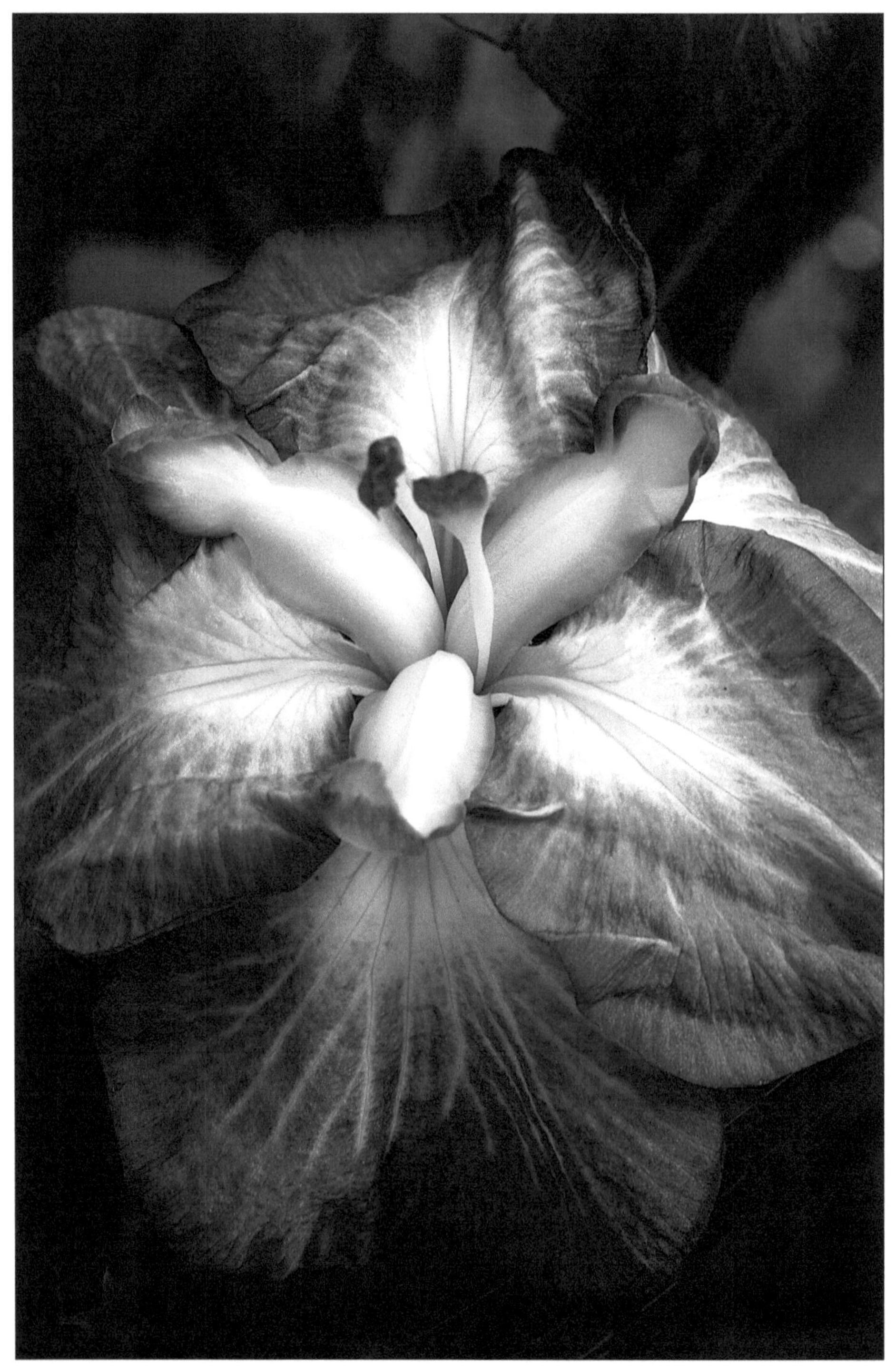

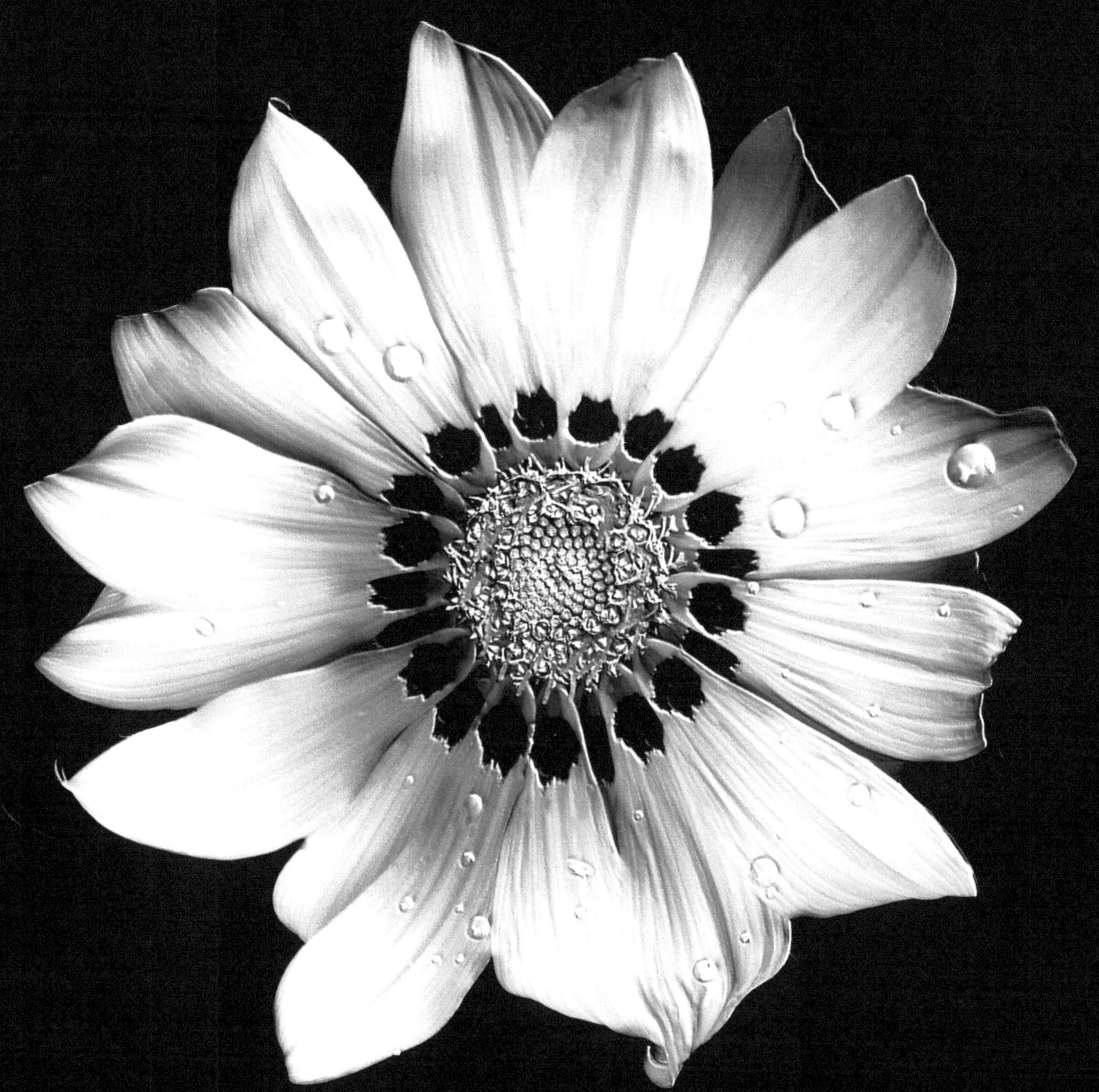

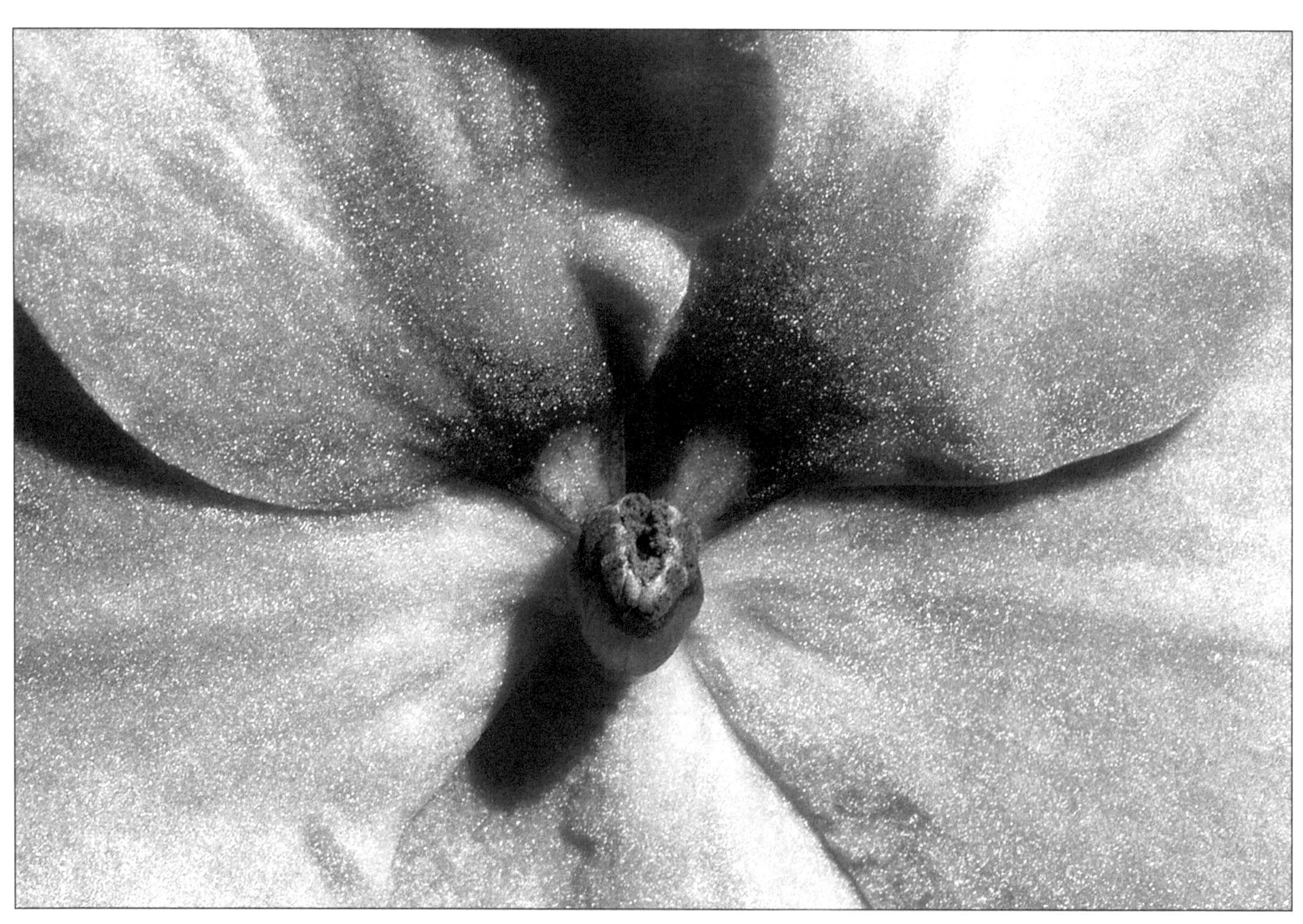

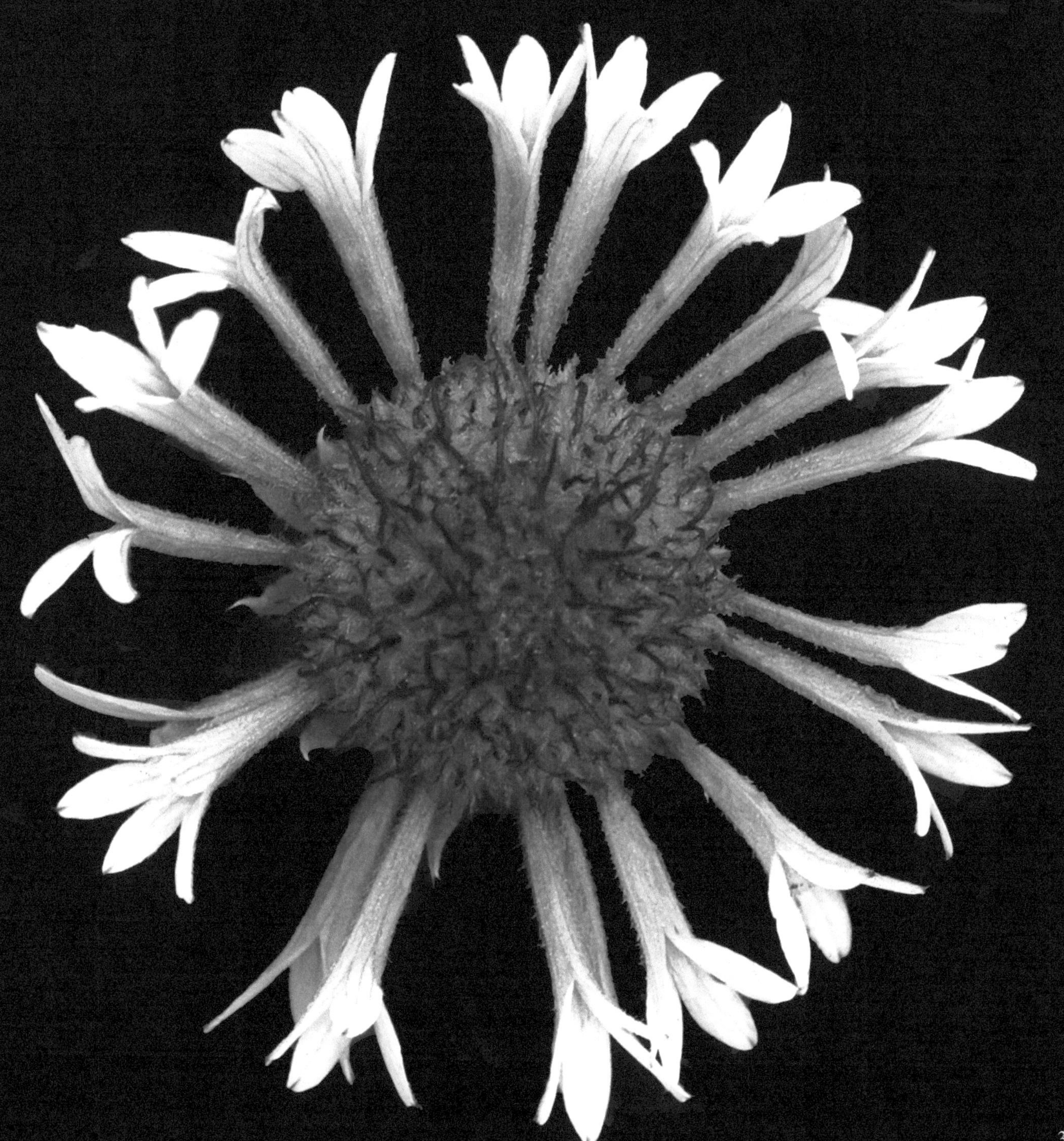

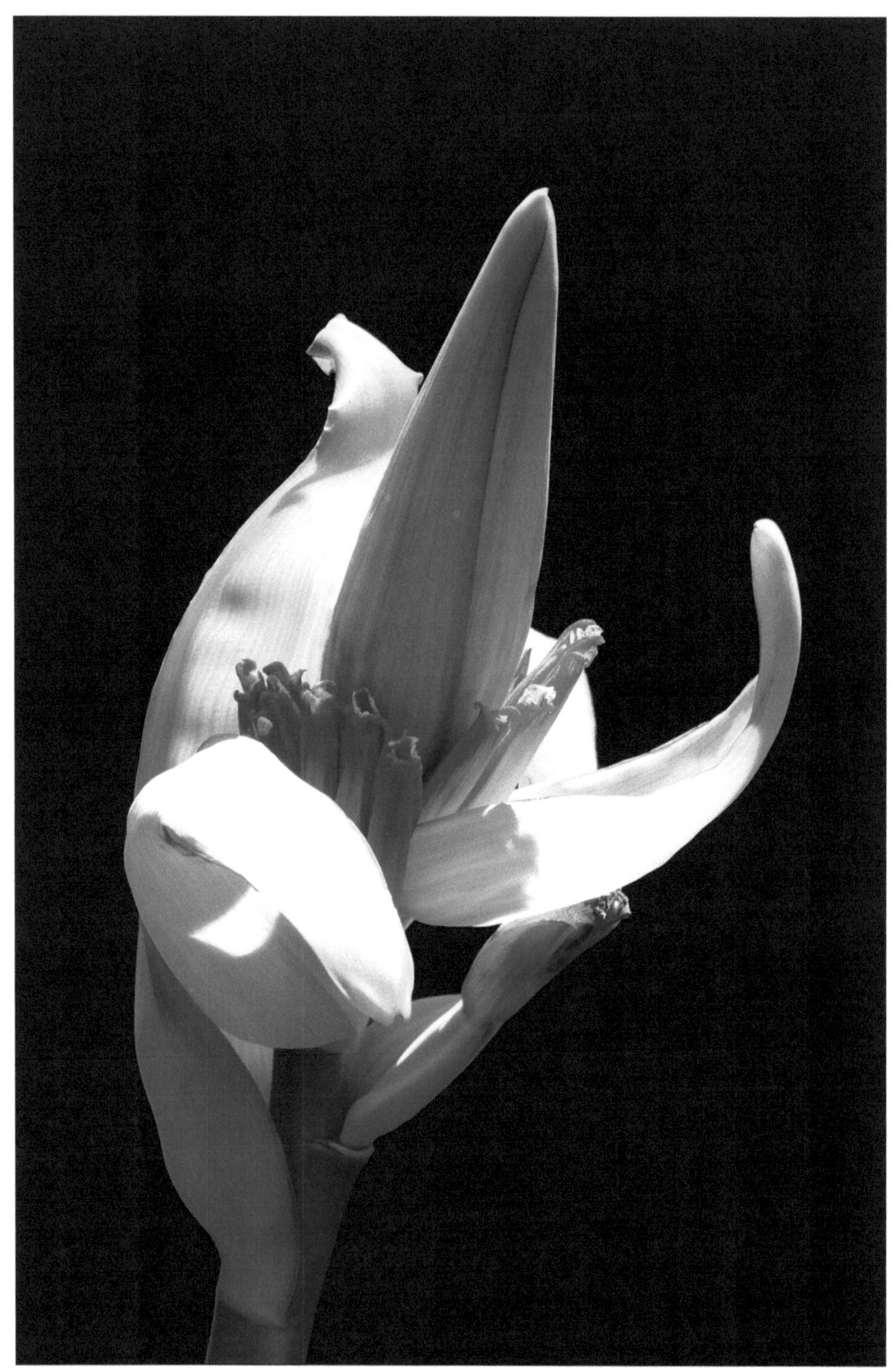

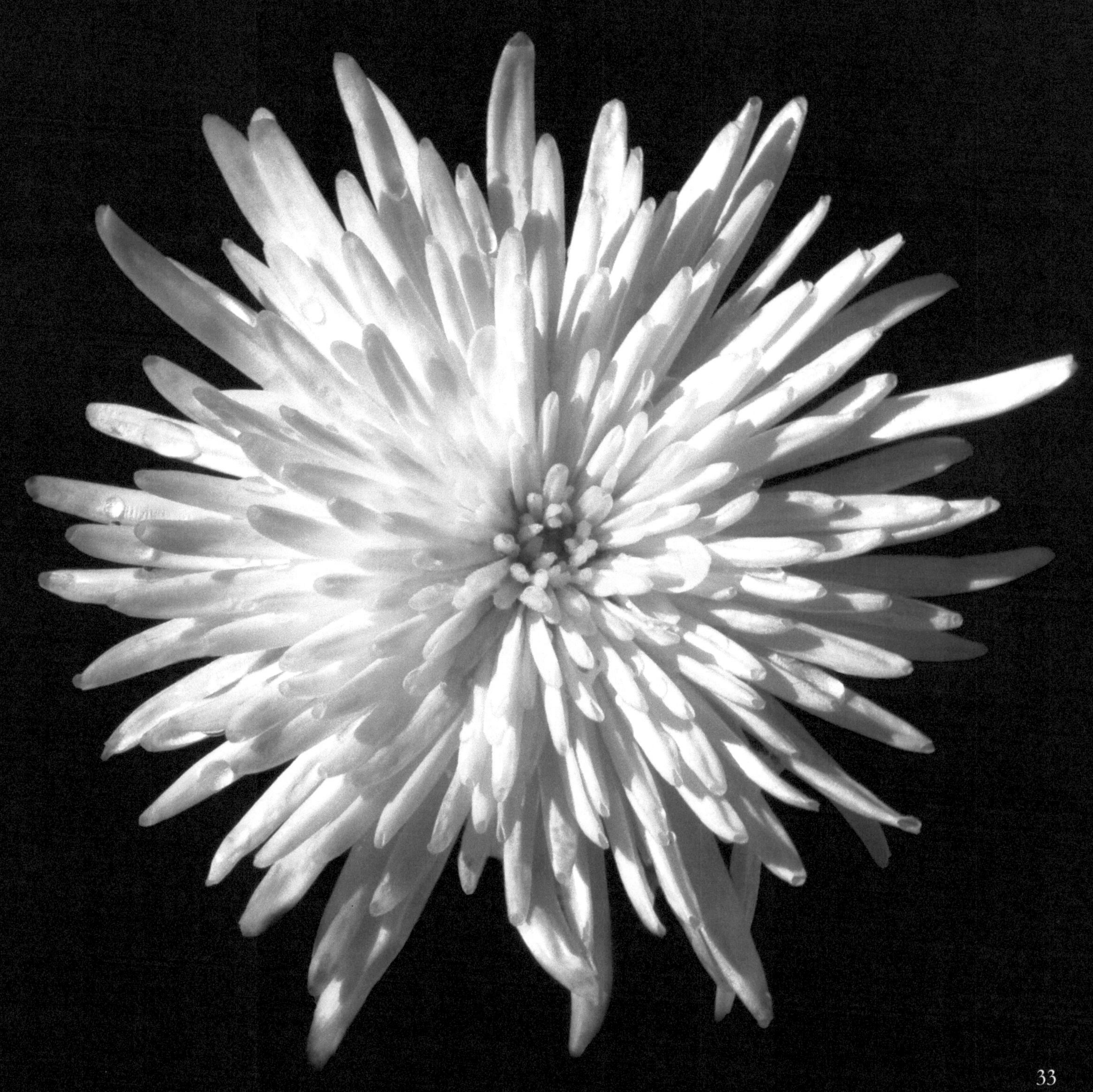

Photographer Bio

BOOKS: R*EJOICE WHEN YOU DIE* - The New Orleans Jazz Funerals
(LSU Press 1998).
PEOPLE AMONG US - Photography by Leo Touchet
(Photo Circle Press 2018)
AT THE RACES - Photography by Leo Touchet
(Photo Circle Press 2018)
CHASING SHADOWS - Desert Sand Dunes
(Photo Circle Press 2018)
DUET - Peot & Photographer - Elizabeth Burk & Leo Touchet
(Yellow Flag Press 2018)

COLLECTIONS: Sir Elton John Photography Collection, New Orelans Museum of Art, Houston Museum of Fine Arts, Bibliotheque National (France), Everson Museum of Art, Schomburg Center (New York Public Library), Chase Manhattan Collection, U.S. National Park Service.

PUBLICATIONS: Life Magazine, Time Magazine, Time Life Books, National Geographic Books, Newsweek Magazine, Fortune Magazine, Natural History Magazine, New York Times, Washington Post, Boston Globe, Oxford American Magazine, Southern Quarterly, Southern Living Magazine, America Illustrated (USIA), Der Stern (Germany), Panorama (Italy), Popular Photography.

EXHIBITIONS: Acadiana Center for the Arts, Arizona State University, Arkansas Art Center, Brooks Memorial (Memphis), Columbus Musuem (Georgia), Everson Museum (Syracuse), Fotofest '92 (Houston), Hofstra University (New York), Louisiana State University, Miami Art Center, Mint Museum (North Carolina), Mississippi Southern University, New Orleans Public Library, Oklahoma Art Center, Public Theater (New York City), Royal Ontario Museum (Toronto), University of Houston, University of Oklahoma, University of Texas.

GROUP EXHIBITIONS:
*REGARDS et MEMOIRES - ARLES 2008 - 39*th Annual Arles, France Photo Expo
(Four Exhibitions including Public Street Banners on the rue de la Roquette)
PHOTOGRAPHY USA 1976, United States Bicentennial Exhibition
(USIA exhibition circulated in the Soviet Union and East Europe).

Leo Touchet's Website: **www.leotouchet.com**

For print sales: Contact Coco Conroy **coco@jacksonfineart.com**
Jackson Fine Art Gallery in Atlanta, Georgia

Photograph Notes

Page - Description

6 - Armonk, New York - *Crocus Blossom 2005*
7 - Armonk, New York *2005*
8 - Abbeville, Louisiana - *Cucumber Blossom 2005*
9 - Armonk, New York *2005*
10 - Armonk, New York - *Dandelion 2005*
11 - New Orleans, Louisiana - *Hibiscus 2003*
12 - Abbeville, Louisiana - *Rose Blossom 2004*
13 - Abbeville, Louisiana - *Rose Blossom 2005*
14 - Armonk, New York - *Daffodil 2005*
15 - Armonk, New York - *Clematis 2005*
16 - Chicago, Illinois - *Lincoln Park 2005*
17 - Abbeville, Louisiana - *Day Lily 2005*
18 - Armonk, New York - *Crocus Blossom 2005*
19 - Bronx, New York - *Botanical Gardens - Water Lily 2012*
20 - Armonk, New York - *Bleeding Heart (Cicentra spectabilis) 2005*
21 - New Orleans, Louisiana *2005*
22 - Armonk, New York - *Snowdrop (Galanthus nivalis) 2005*
23 - Chicago, Illinois - *Lincoln Park 2005*
24 - St. Augustine, Florida *2005*
25 - Ontario, Canada *2005*
26 - Armonk, New York -*Orchid 2004*
27 - Armonk, New York - *Bearded Iris 2005*
28 - Bronx, New York - *Botanical Gardens - Monet Exhibit 2012*
29 - Armonk, New York *2004*
30 - Quebec, Canada *2013*
31 - Chicago, Illinois - *Lincoln Park 2005*
32 - St. Martin Parish, Louisiana - *Banana Blossom 2018*
33 - Abbeville, Louisiana *2004*

Other Photo Books by
LEO TOUCHET

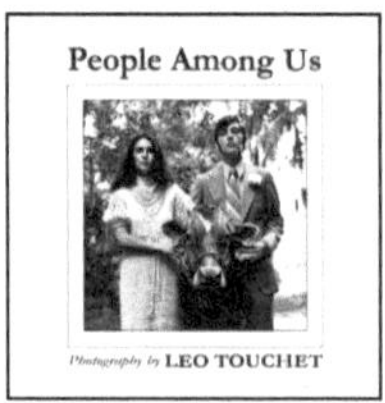

People Among Us - *Photography by Leo Touchet*

ISBN: 9781732443303 - 8.5 x 8.5 inches - 46 Pages - Paperback
Black & white photographs of people around the world.

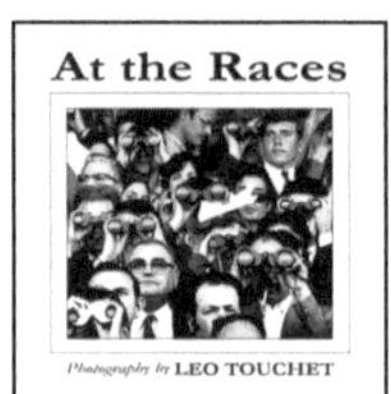

At The Races - *Photography by Leo Touchet*

ISBN: 9781732443310 - 8.5 x 8.5 inches - 42 Pages - Paperback
Black & white photographs of people at horse race tracks.

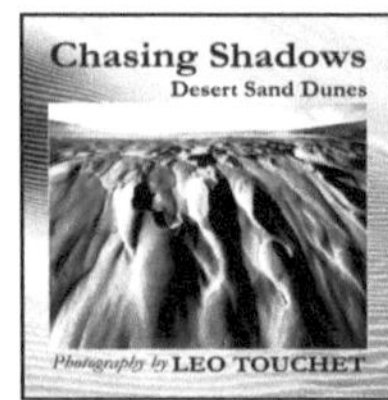

Chasing Shadows - *Desert Sand Dunes*

ISBN: 9781732443303 - 8.5 x 8.5 inches - 36 Pages - Paperback
Black & white photographs of desert sand dunes.

These books are available from:

www.photocirclepress.com

www.ingramcontent.com/pod-product-compliance
Lightning Source LLC
LaVergne TN
LVHW070159110826
845147LV00002B/451

* 9 7 8 1 7 3 2 4 4 3 3 3 4 *